THE PACESETTERS:
ADVISORY

The best practice guide
for accountancy firms

Acknowledgements

Firstly, we'd like to thank the extraordinary personnel of our pacesetting practices for giving us your time and valuable insights. This book wouldn't be what it is without each and every one of you. Thanks also to our accounting industry contributors - you are the experts in this space, and you deserve your place in this book.

A very special thank-you is due to the Xero team who helped get this book together. A book is a huge task and it takes a team to bring it to life. Anna Curzon, Xero's chief partner and product officer, unfailingly believed in this project and championed it from idea to completion. Caitlin Clarke produced the book and made it happen - without her, it wouldn't exist. Andrea Philippou created another amazing design and layout for the book. Many other people both in and out of Xero helped out enormously, and we'd like to extend our gratitude to all of them.

Thanks are also due to our excellent legal and proofreading teams, without whom there'd be a lot more errors in the book. Any that remain are solely ours.

We couldn't have done it without all your help, so thanks again

- Josh Drummond and Doug LaBahn

CONTENTS

FOREWORD

By Anna Curzon, Chief Product and Partner Officer, Xero

First, thank you so much for reading this book. It's my hope that these case studies of some of our extraordinary pacesetting practices, and the amazing advice from a selection of the top thought leaders in the advisory space, will be of help to you and your practice on your advisory journey.

Many of you will be here because you've already moved your practice over to the cloud, or you've started the process. If you have, you'll have experienced first-hand how embracing the cloud creates greater efficiency. You've given yourselves the gift of time you wouldn't otherwise have, and you've got extra capacity to take on advisory work.

Or do you? As you've probably experienced, nature abhors a vacuum, and work *always* expands to fill the time available. Most accountants we talk to are as busy as ever. They've backfilled that time with things like longer, more complex jobs, new clients, staff coaching, and more involved compliance work. Many still find themselves too busy to focus on the future.

Taking the time to read books like this is a great opportunity to jump forward by learning from other practices, and to look ahead and clarify where you want to go over the next couple of years. While you can of course try things on your own, we've found that learning from others is the fastest path forward.

The pacesetting practices in this book have a solid grip on their business model and laser-sharp clarity of vision for the firm's future. This includes the services they offer clients, the technology they select, the staff education programs, and skills needed to execute their strategy.

That doesn't mean they're perfect – in fact, everyone we spoke to for this book was very quick to point out that they're far from it! But as you'll see, they've been brave enough to make mistakes and learn lessons along the way. That's the reason they're in this book; to offer the benefit of their advisory experiences for others.

Because, for every firm that has made the decision not to focus *purely* on compliance, offering more advisory services is a must.

So, because it's one of the most important questions in the industry, and everyone is asking it: what do we really mean by 'advisory'?

Accountants have been offering advisory services for a long time in a variety of ways, perhaps as a bespoke service for the companies that can afford it, as ad-hoc advice, or too often, as an unpaid extra service. In the past, really comprehensive advisory was often enormously resource-intensive and as a result, many advisory services were expensive, and usually only available to larger companies that could afford them.

All that has changed. In much the same way as tech giants like Google and Facebook have enabled small businesses to have a market presence they never would have dreamed of in the pre-internet days, the advent of cloud accounting has brought the cost of financial data collection and analysis way down.

This means small businesses can now expect the quality of advice only big companies could command in the past. And these businesses are desperate to get meaningful advice to help them survive and thrive in the new economy. Who will provide this to them?

The answer is you. You, and other forward-thinking, pacesetting accounting firms. You already have the foundation of advisory services – accurate, reliable, trusted data – through the compliance work you do on the Xero cloud platform. Offering more advisory services to a market that's hungry for it is the next big step for the accounting and bookkeeping industry, and Xero is here to support you all the way.

Anna Curzon
Chief Product and Partner Officer
Xero

INTRODUCTION

By Josh Drummond and Doug LaBahn

When we started work on what would become the first Xero-published book, *The Pacesetters*, we did so because there was a perception in the accounting industry that existing books and other materials were long on the "why" of concepts like cloud and digital transformation for accountants, and short on the "how." Conversely, there was plenty of material available on how to actually *operate* cloud accounting software, but there was far less content on how practices themselves could manage the human side of the cloud transformation.

We realised that the answer was right in front of us: our work at Xero gives us incredible access to the top performing cloud practices in the accounting industry. Who better for accountants and bookkeepers to learn from than the best firms across NZ, AU, UK, US, Canada and around the world?

The Pacesetters has since become a success, despite being written primarily for the UK market, and (at the time of writing) the book has already had its third print run. The level of interest around the book from the day it was first published has shown that there's a big appetite in the market for insightful, actionable content that showcases the on-the-ground experiences of real accounting and bookkeeping practices. It's our hope that this book, and those that follow, will play their part in spreading success throughout the Xero partner community and beyond.

When *The Pacesetters* first came out, one of the most common requests we had from readers was for more advisory content. With the amount of interest in the subject, it made perfect sense to write the next Xero-published the book about it. But we were cautious, not least because advisory is a much debated topic in accounting industry. We have more than once seen, heard, (or overheard) variations on the phrase "advisory is bullshit". Sure, it's most often uttered by hard-bitten cynical types, but there's no doubt that the concept is contentious. There are good reasons for this. The changes that digitisation and cloud software have wrought in accounting are real, they are happening fast, and some people in the industry feel like their livelihoods are threatened. Some cynicism about a new thing that is often perceived to be about replacing compliance work and ushering in a brave new world is to be expected.

There are other psychological factors at play, too. There's no one "right" way to do advisory, and future outcomes are always uncertain. This, and the need to become fluent in a potential myriad of client businesses, shakes many accountants to their core, used as they are to the more reliable world of compliance where they only need to be experts in the rules laid out by the authorities. Compliance is about following well-documented rules, fact-finding and calculating hard numbers. A lot of accounting's bread and butter is applied knowledge and maths, becoming faster and more efficient at repetitive tasks, and there's a real comfort in that. No matter how uncertain things are in other ways, 2+2 always equals 4, and taxes are still as certain as death itself.

However, it's also this reliable nature that makes the more mathematical, repetitive aspects of compliance easily automated. Why this is a problem quickly becomes apparent when you look at the recent history of accounting. Many, if not most, accounting practices over the last half-century or so have invested enormous energy and resources into, essentially, turning their practices into factories and their staff into robots. In this world, staff are often most prized for the speed and accuracy with which they can complete work; it's a given that said work is reliable, and repetitive; and time is tracked in and charged in six-minute increments. In this world, where chargeables are everything, client interaction is often a genuine nuisance, something that gets in the way of actually getting the work done. Little wonder that traditional practice structures have been engineered to ensure clients are kept well away from staff, and vice versa.

Advisory is turning that world completely upside-down. Practices have to demonstrate to clients why their work is valuable, rather than having clients arrive on a conveyor belt of compliance legislation; client interaction is not just allowed, but encouraged. Juniors (not just partners!) meet with the heads of multi-million-dollar businesses and – worst of all – the work deals not just with the concrete reality of the past but the explicitly uncertain future.

No wonder some accountants balk at this juncture. It's often the opposite of everything they know.

Of course, the best antidote to cynicism or apprehension is a working example. Luckily, we have lots.

This book is a mixture of particularly in-depth case studies that shine a light on pacesetting Xero practices, and advice from some of the best minds in the accounting thought leadership, education and app development fields – many of whom have identified successful advisory practices and authored books themselves. Every case study features its own set of focus questions and key action items to help you utilise lessons from our pacesetters.

It's worth noting at this point that the opinions and experiences in this book may not always line up neatly with each other, and that's to be expected. Ask six different accountants about time-tracking, for example, and you'll get six (or more) different answers. That being said, this book is about showcasing the common themes of the most successful ideas and repeatable actions (of which there are many) rather than highlighting differences in approach (which are less important).

Advisory is simple, but it's not easy. At its heart, it's simply about helping people – but in practice, and at scale, it can also be about rethinking and transforming the way an accounting practice operates from the ground up.

We hope this book will help you with helping clients, with practice transformation, and everything in between.

Josh Drummond and Doug LaBahn, Ph.D.

One more thing...

We'd like all our readers to feel as involved and included as possible in the books, and other content, that we're writing.

The extraordinary stories and case studies in this book are only a very small slice of the incredible expertise and brilliant work done every day by hundreds of pacesetting practices. Rather than highlight small parts of many different practices, we've instead chosen to take an extra in-depth look at a single practice in each region that Xero currently operates in.

However, we're extremely aware that there are many, many more practices out there that are more than worthy of inclusion in this book, and we want to be able to include them as well.

To do that – guided by the way we make Xero itself – we decided to take a leaf out of the software development book. So, please think of this book as version 1.0 of a much bigger project. We aim to update this book over time as we interview more pacesetters, receive further worthy contributions, and acquire new insights. **Most importantly, we will be incorporating reader feedback**. In today's world, there's no reason why a book shouldn't be as frequently updated, or as guided by customer feedback, as a piece of software.

We'd love our books to be a two-way conversation, so please send any and all feedback on this, or any of our books, to **pacesetters@xero.com**. If you think we've got something slightly, or even entirely wrong; if we've shared only part of the picture and you have the rest of it; if you think we've done a great job but could stand to take another viewpoint into account; if you've got a great candidate for a case study, or even if you think the spotlight should be shone on your own thought leadership or accounting practice! Thanks to reader input, we anticipate ebook versions will receive regular updates in the near future, and we'll make sure the changes are all rolled up into any future print editions. So tell us what you think. We'll read every email, and we can't wait to hear from you.

Email your thoughts and feedback on this book to **pacesetters@xero.com**

01

THE MEANING
OF 'ADVISORY'

Advisory can be a tricky term. For all the accountants proudly talking about how offering advisory services has opened up new avenues of profitability and job satisfaction in their practices, there are many others who are struggling to get to grips with what the term actually means, or who view the utopian promises (or vendor pitches) sometimes associated with the word with an entirely understandable scepticism.

The problem with the term seems to be that it's broad, vague, and hard to pin down to any one job or definition, so it means different things to different people. The way advisory is sometimes seen as a sort of threat to, or replacement for, the compliance services that are many firms' bread and butter doesn't always help. What many accountants feel when advisory is spoken of, is something to the effect of "Okay, so the more basic tax work I do won't be as valuable in the future. I can understand that. But what is this thing that's meant to be replacing it? And how do I do it?"

To help clear up these muddied waters, we talked to Paul Bulpitt of The Wow Company – who, like many accountants, is dubious about the ways that the term "advisory" gets bandied around.

"It's a bit like the Emperor's new clothes. Everyone's talking about it, but it's just really clear that so many firms don't know what advisory is," Paul says. But there's a way forward, because advisory, at a basic level, can be easily defined – and you can build on it from there.

"In my experience, clients want someone who understands their personal situation, and helps them reach their goals – but sometimes, this might just be me showing them a way that they don't have to spend their entire Sunday afternoon, or one whole weekend a month, doing their accounts. Showing you how they don't have to do that, showing them how to do it better – for me, that's advisory."

Paul says there's a real quest for relevance among many accounting firms, and that quest can be fulfilled by understanding what their customers' needs and wants are, and offering helpful services to suit. Many clients want more than just a year-end summation of their accounts; they want someone who can be on hand to offer financial advice, and who can help them run their businesses better. He suggests that rather than racing to offer advisory services to shore up compliance offerings, that accountants first look at why they got into the business in the first place, and *then* look at the expanded services they can offer.

"The one thing that you can say for pretty much every accountant that I've ever met is that they're good people and they want to help people," Paul says.

"I know this is a bit out there, but the bit of advice I'd give for accountants wanting to do advisory is reconnect with that desire to help people, and to drill down into what helping people actually means. To give them reassurance over their numbers and make [that job] easier for them. Even as the world's getting more and more automated, globally, we've got more and more regulation. How can we, as accountants and advisors, make it easier for clients to get the information they need?"

So what does advisory mean? It's just another way of saying "helping people". If accountants, whether they call themselves advisors or not, can concentrate on that, rather than the disputed or controversial meaning of a particular term, then the term itself ceases to matter quite as much, and it doesn't really matter whether you call it advisory, business advice, or anything else. It might be a debate among accountants, but if it's not one that clients care about, or that advances their interests, then perhaps it's best not worried about.

All that said, it can be helpful to place a bit of structure around how we're using the term in this book, so we've broken things down a bit further.

The core differences between compliance and advisory services

The simplest way to answer the question of which services are advisory and which are compliance is to look at whether the services focus on the future or the past.

Compliance is made up of services that **look back in time**. Tax returns, year-end or monthly accounts – these are all snapshots of the past. They deal with known facts and figures.

Advisory services, on the other hand, **look at either the present or the future**. Advice, while it is usually based on what is currently happening, as well as what's happened in the past, is **always about what to do in the future**.

Any of your existing future-focused or planning services can be grouped under the banner of 'advisory' services.

Compliance services	• Look at the past • Driven by needs
Advisory services	• Looks to the past to analyse the present • Future-focused • Driven by wants

THE VITAL ROLE OF BOOKKEEPING

Compliance, through bookkeeping, can be often foundational to offering advisory - when it's paired with the cloud.

Depending on the industry, there are a number of different definitions for what constitutes quality data. For accounting, the definition of good data is usually that it is accurate, reliable and complete. This is the essence of good bookkeeping practice, and it's a concept that accountants will find themselves right at home with; it's about *getting it right*.

The good news is that this familiar aspect of accounting is also essential for the less-comfortable world of future-focused advisory. To do advisory, you require accurate, reliable and complete data, just as you do for compliance, and all other aspects of accounting practice.

This is where the cloud comes in. When you pair bookkeeping with the cloud, you're *automatically* creating a platform for advisory. The data's all in one place, and when everything has been set up properly, it's not only accurate, reliable and complete; it's also timely, and relevant to clients. Even if you've only used the cloud to do yearly compliance, the data gathered can be used for advice. And with the cloud's single ledger, it's now easier than ever to start a profitable bookkeeping sideline, or to outsource bookkeeping services, and leverage the data for advisory.

Nearly every pacesetting advisory practice we speak to in this book thinks of compliance and bookkeeping as utterly foundational to offering advisory services. Many of them offer in-house bookkeeping services as part of their advisory service packages. Other, more advisory-focused practices outsource their bookkeeping, but the data is still vital to their advisory offering.

STRUCTURING ADVISORY SERVICES

There is no 100 percent correct way to group or structure advisory services, and there are a variety of models on the market. Several of these models will be referred to in different chapters of this book. However, often the most appealing and easy-to-understand models are the simplest, so that's the main direction we take. Here's how we will refer to compliance and advisory throughout this book.

We label past-focused services, or those that revolve around staying legal and compliant, "compliance".

Everything that's focused on an analysis of the present state, or that looks to the future, can be labelled as "advisory."

We can then partition these future-focused advisory services into two service models or revenue streams: simple advisory (also called business advisory) and complex advisory.

Please note that these names and this structure isn't meant to be representative of a hierarchy or even a preferable progression for firms. No one model is "better" than another; it's simply a way of structuring different services. Simple advisory isn't always simple; it's just that the skills required tend to be within more people's reach. Likewise, complex advisory is not intrinsically "better" than simple advisory, although it does usually take more specialised skills to perform. Also, it's important to realise that this spectrum isn't set in stone. The different service models tend to bleed into each other. The spectrum also varies by client. For instance, jobs that more usually fit into "complex advisory" will sometimes be simpler, for a client with less complex needs.

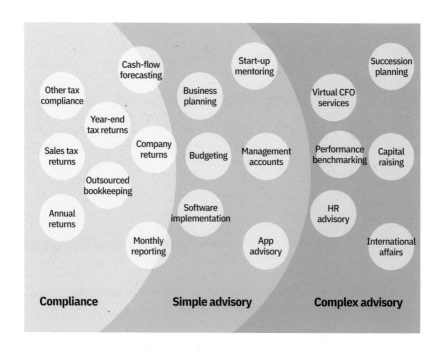

The first model – compliance – encompasses firms that focus primarily on helping clients meet their compliance obligations on time, accurately and efficiently. These practices often find their processes become more efficient when they switch to cloud accounting. However, they can find it challenging to increase the proportion of advisory work because their teams are so focused on compliance, and they fall back into doing what they've always done.

The second model – simple advisory – is for firms that have a strong appreciation of technology and an awareness that the majority of their clients need reasonably-priced services in addition to compliance – like cash flow forecasting, budgeting, and planning – requiring both automation and accounting insights. Simple advisory is also commonly referred to as "business advisory."

The third model – complex advisory – is common in both well-established, larger firms and boutique advisory businesses with a reputation of successfully navigating businesses through the intricacies of the full business life-cycle. For example, they specialise in complex expertise, international transactions, or complex multi-jurisdictional regulations. Firms focusing on this revenue stream place priority on finding, nurturing and retaining experts, understanding that their skills are key to the firm's success.

EXERCISE: WHERE ARE YOU AT WITH ADVISORY?

There's a good chance that your firm is already offering a number of these advisory services. However, most accounting firms are not yet set up to optimally deliver advisory services at scale. As a rough average across the industry, firms spend around 80 percent of their time doing compliance, and maybe 20 percent on advisory.

However you're currently operating, we understand that it's a challenge to change, which is why we've created the exercises below to help you get a high-level view of your current performance. You can use the results to benchmark your future performance, to help you be aware of progress over time.

WHERE DO YOUR REVENUES COME FROM CURRENTLY?

This exercise will help you identify current service models in your firm. The questions come from our global benchmarking research, where respondents were asked to identify the services from which they derived the most revenue for their practice.

Compliance services	Currently offering? Mark yes/no	Revenues List approximate revenues p/a, and note revenues that are a substantial proportion of practice income – Xero data indicates that over £40k revenue p/a indicates a sustainable service line for the average practice.	Can our team offer this service in a way that's valuable to clients, while remaining profitable? Mark yes/no
Accounting			
Bookkeeping			
Tax preparation services			
Payroll services			
Compliance work (e.g. GST F5 preparation, unaudited financial statements, other compliance work)			
Accounts receivable / control services			

Simple advisory services	Currently offering? Mark yes/no	Revenues List approximate revenues p/a, and note revenues that are a substantial proportion of practice income – Xero data indicates that over £40k revenue p/a indicates a sustainable service line for the average practice.	Can our team offer this service in a way that's valuable to clients, while remaining profitable? Mark yes/no
Forecasting, budgeting, cash flow and business planning, etc.			
Startup mentoring, advice and networking/ assistance with business development			
For-fee implementations of accounting software for businesses that are unlikely to become long-term client of your firm			
Tax advisory			

Complex advisory services	Currently offering? Mark yes/no	Revenues List approximate revenues p/a, and note revenues that are a substantial proportion of practice income – Xero data indicates that over £40k revenue p/a indicates a sustainable service line for the average practice.	Can our team offer this service in a way that's valuable to clients, while remaining profitable? Mark yes/no
Virtual or outsourced CFO services			
Capital raising / assistance moving to better interest / terms / financing options			
Succession planning services			
Business app/software (other than accounting) setup, configuration and support services			
Business performance benchmarking			

Focus exercise: Of all these services, if you could only focus on three to achieve your revenue goals, what would they be?

This question is an excellent discussion point to put to the whole practice. Where does your expertise lie? What do your staff most like doing? Could you achieve your revenue goals by focusing more on particular services? And, if not, what services might need to be built, or rebuilt, to deliver the most value to clients, staff and the practice?

Now, take a minute to break down your revenues by percentage for each service model.

This will give you a snapshot of how your firm is currently performing when it comes to advisory in general terms, which you can come back to later to see how things have changed.

Compliance _____%

Simple Advisory _____%

Complex Advisory _____%

HOW DO YOUR CLIENTS SEE YOUR SERVICES?

It's important to be honest with yourself when answering this question. Do your clients think of you as someone who provides forward-looking advice, or do they think of you as someone who prepares historical, annual accounts once a year and tells them how much tax they have to pay?

If you surveyed your small business clients, how would they rate you, on a scale of 1 to 10, as an advisor? (10 = best possible rating, 1 = worst possible rating.)

On average, clients would rate my services _____ out of 10.

Would clients say you've made a huge difference to how they run their business?

Yes | No | Mixed

Why is this?

Do clients ask for your advice on a regular basis?
Yes | No | Mixed

Where would 80% of your clients rate you on the scale below?

LOOKING BACK AND PREPARING NUMBERS

LOOKING FORWARD WITH REGULAR, HELPFUL ADVICE

| 1 | 2 | 3 | 4 | 5 | 6 | 7 | 8 | 8 | 10 |

Where you land on this scale will give you a rough idea of how much you are currently focusing on offering advisory services as a firm. If you don't know enough about what clients think to make an educated guess, then the next step might be asking them to find out.

02

FINDING THE PATH TO HIGH PERFORMANCE

By Doug LaBahn

The tools and mindset to help achieve 'Time Better Spent' in your practice.

What's the best way to get your practice performing as well as possible, as quickly as possible?

While it remains true that there are no shortcuts to success, data analysis tells us a lot about what successful practices have in common. The good news here is that the path to high performance has never been so clearly marked.

Josh and I are very fortunate to have access to information on tens of thousands of accounting and bookkeeping firms, as well as the opportunity to spend time searching out and documenting the best practices of... well, the best practices!

These are the firms where staff and management are able to do their best work, and their clients are receiving the support and coaching they need to move their businesses forward. When you see practices combining the best of technology with the best of accounting and finance, it's a powerful thing to witness.

In *The Pacesetters* we shared the blueprint for firms to follow for moving their practices to the cloud. Now, we're pleased to present the best practices for capturing the advisory service opportunity that's right in front of you. The success stories and information we're sharing is actionable, and well within your reach.

We started this project thinking that it might be challenging to identify the foundation of scaled, sustainable advisory services. We rolled up our sleeves and dug into the details, tapping into the vast database of partner performance data that underpins our Industry Benchmarking reports, the longitudinal data at the core of our Xero platform, and the hundreds of partner success stories we've captured in narrative and video format.

What we found was surprising, both in its simplicity and in terms of the sheer strength of evidence, in every market where our partners operate.

Figure 1 shows the progression of technology adoption across the continuum from practices that are far behind (A) to the average practice today (B), to the best-performing, pacesetting firms (C). For example, eighty-nine percent of pacesetters identified in our 2018 Australia and New Zealand Industry reports fall at point C in the figure. In contrast, 68 percent of all practices surveyed fall between A and B, with the remainder turning the corner and moving toward point C.

The essentials for capturing the simple advisory services opportunity

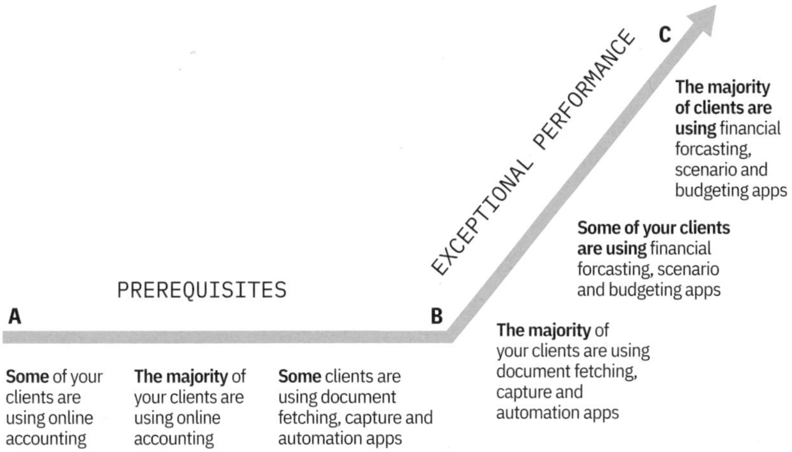

Figure 1. The essentials for capturing the simple advisory services opportunity

HOW PACESETTERS FOUND A BETTER WAY

The leaders of pacesetting firms have figured out that clients don't value the many hours accountants and bookkeepers spend on creating and then error-checking spreadsheets. They've realised that spreadsheets are great when used for bespoke or highly customised data analysis, but are bad for data collection.

They also know that once data is extracted from their accounting software, its accuracy starts decaying at an alarming rate, as new transactions and entries in the accounting system are ignored by the 'snapshot' of the business in the spreadsheet.

Pacesetting partners were early to recognise the importance of having a single, regularly-updated, source of information. They know that it's this that fuels effective collaboration with their clients. This is what led them to be the earliest adopters of online accounting powered by automatic ingestion and coding of bank feeds.

Their next ambition was to automatically capture, classify and store the documents small businesses create as they run their business. As a result, they quickly adopted apps like Receipt Bank, Hubdoc, Auto Entry and Datamolino. Business owners, bookkeepers and accountants began to really love these apps for the time they saved from having to do what they thought of as boring data entry processes. In addition, the accuracy, completeness and timeliness of accounting information increased by leaps and bounds. What bank feeds did for online accounting, these apps took to the next level by turning on automatic document and bill feeds.

The proven cloud technologies adopted by pacesetting firms work on two levels. **They give accountants and bookkeepers extra time**, which can be better spent, and they offer informational and scenario-based **tools that enable them to have rich and rewarding discussions with clients.**

HOW THE ESSENTIALS UNLOCK THE ADVISORY
SERVICE OPPORTUNITY

Blockers	Proven Technologies	Efficiencies Realised	Exceptional Performance
Using desktop accounting software, or boxes of receipts and bank statements	Having nearly all of yourclients using onlineaccounting software	You, your staff and your clients all work with the same realtime information	∧ Client retention ∧ Client referrals
Chasing clients for mundane documents to finalise their accounts and lodgements	Having nearly all of yourclients using apps thatautomate the fetching and capture of receipts, bills and documents	You, your staff and your clients are given back all the time that is wasted on the boring process of finding, entering and validating information	∧ Employee excitement, engagement, growth and value creation
Spending hours in spreadsheets and not knowing if the formulas are free of errors	Having the majority of your clients using apps that let you set up up forecasts, budgets and scenarios forthem and having the automatically update the information as it comes in	You, your staff and your clients can open any browser, review progress and discuss what the business can and can't do	∧ Revenue per client ∧ Profitability

Figure 2. outlines why this works so well
across so many practices.

TIME BETTER SPENT

Pacesetting practices "fail fast". Pacesetting accounting and bookkeeping firms are fun to watch because they quickly test and grade apps. They're ruthless about discarding apps that don't deliver better outcomes for their clients, staff and business. These exceptional firms have purposely used technology to free up the time to spend more time with clients.

Pacesetting practices focus on the future when they talk with their clients. The client interactions of the best-performing practices are founded on up-to-date information and are centred on offering advice for the future of the business. This is a dramatic shift from the old model of client interaction, where conversations centred on completing compliance tasks that look to the past, and are of lesser interest to business owners. Instead, pacesetting accountants and bookkeepers find they are most valued when they collaborate with clients about what they should or should not do with their business, based upon their current and forecasted financial positions.

DOES THIS REALLY WORK?

Most accountants and bookkeepers will agree that using cloud accounting and apps will free up some time in their practice, but may query whether their clients will see the value, or whether their firms will be able to perform at a level that makes the investment worth it.

We wanted to be sure that these findings were applicable across the board, so we went a step further and ran the numbers against our survey database of 5,500 participating accounting and bookkeeping firms to see what differences we would find for these groups across different levels of app use.

Figure 3 shows what we found. The higher the use of data automation apps in a practice, and the more clients on cloud accounting software, the more time is freed up.

The trend is equally visible in the opposite direction; practices with fewer clients on online accounting, and a lower uptake of data automation apps, find themselves spending more hours per client per year, and they have much less free time.

USE OF DATA AUTOMATION APPS

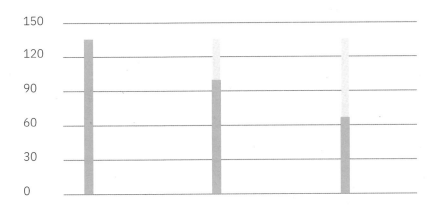

USE OF FINANCIAL FORECASTING, BUDGETING AND SCENARIO APPS

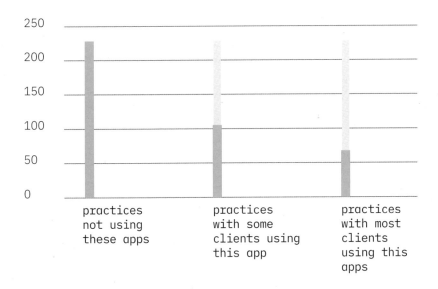

time available to do other things

average time per client

INVISIBLE VS VISIBLE TIME

But there's a seeming paradox here; isn't the whole idea to be able to spend *more* time on clients?

This apparent contradiction is resolved by the fact that practices with better cloud adoption are able to spend more quality, *visible* time with clients. While the actual per-client time spend is lower, what that amounts to is fewer "invisible" hours spent in data entry and validation (but which the client is still billed for!) and more "visible" hours spent giving clients the forward-focused advice that's truly valuable to their business. Clients don't care how many hours you spend getting their numbers right; they only care about results. This also explains why these practices are stickier; clients are far more likely to retain the services of a practice where they can actively see and experience the value being offered.

Cloud and app adoption make practices better places to work, as well. The practice staff and partners we spoke to in 1-on-1 interviews often describe their new-found ability to spend more time giving advice, building personal relationships, and enjoy seeing their clients achieve results, while having a lot more fun at the same time.

So can every practice do this?

We believe that virtually any practice, from sole practitioners to the largest firms, can achieve time better spent by making greater use of the technologies widely available today.

If you're leaning toward believing that only a few, highly-specialised or brand-new firms can make use of the app and data automation opportunity offered by the cloud accounting platform, I'd challenge you to square that opinion with the following facts:

- **Data automation apps make up the number one category of apps** in the Xero ecosystem, with the greatest number of connections to Xero orgs.

- **Financial forecasting, budgeting and scenario apps make up the number two app category** ranked on connections to Xero orgs.

At the time of writing, over 2,350 practices have over 50 percent of their Xero business edition clients using data automation apps, and nearly 1,100 practices have over fifty percent of their clients using financial forecasting, budgeting and scenario apps.

These numbers lead us to believe that just starting to use these apps will be enough to drive efficiencies in the firms that are brave enough to give it a proper go.

Focus questions

Through our research in this area, we've learned a few key questions that you'll need to ask yourself and the other leaders in your practice.

1. **Are you willing to be authentic?** When we ask pacesetting practices for their advice to accountants and bookkeepers who are just starting on their journey to capture the advisory services opportunity, their advice is simple and direct: **You must use these apps for your own practice**. It's really clear that if you're not using these apps, then you and your staff will constantly struggle and stumble when you're trying to sell or deliver simple advisory services, like financial forecasting and budgeting services, to clients. To truly understand the benefits and potential of these apps, you need to be using them and have first-hand experience setting them up, learning their nuances and making decisions using the realtime information they provide.

2. **Are you committed to making the lives of your team better?** Take your team out for a couple of drinks and ask them if they enjoy data entry or whether time spent building / rebuilding / checking spreadsheets is enjoyable. If they're honest, they will say the work is boring, tedious and unlikely to create real value for clients. They know that technology can and should do more in these areas. So, you have to make the tough choice to change – or else there's a very good chance your team will make the easy choice to move on another more enjoyable career opportunity.

3. **Are you curious and courageous?** Pacesetting firms all seem to share the same quality. They're relentlessly focused on helping their clients achieve their personal definitions of success. They love giving their clients a clear picture of what's ahead for their businesses and working with

them to know what they can and can't do in their business. Their energy flows from a deep well of curiosity and hope. They know that they will be asked tough questions by clients and that it's always possible that the advice they give may not be followed, or may not turn out as expected or hoped. Even so, they power forward. New ways to achieve time better spent, and better ways to work together with clients are always on the horizon, and they are so curious and courageous that they'll take the leap of faith and go for it.

If you answered *"yes"* to all three and are not already right up there with the pacesetters, here's the best path to follow with the greatest odds of success.

THE SIMPLE STAIRCASE TO SUCCESS NEARLY EVERYONE FOLLOWS

AND FINALLY...

Two last bits of advice to help you on your journey to unlock the opportunities right in front of you. First, have fun! There are so many new and interesting apps and clients. Once you embrace these technologies you'll have lots of time to better spend enjoying what you love to do. Second, find some other advisors to learn from and explore these opportunities together. One of the sayings at home when I was growing up was "many hands make light work, and many minds make smart work". Please let us know how it's going for you and what you're learning along the way – we always want to hear from you.

03

THE FIVE PHASES OF BUSINESS ADVISORY SUCCESS

By James Mason, Managing Director, Mindshop

Visit the website of any progressive accounting firm and the service line 'Business Advisory', or more broadly, just 'Advisory', will appear. This 'catch-all' definition often causes confusion on many fronts – to customers, prospects and most importantly, team members and clients – and so it begs some questions:

- What is advisory?

- What advisory services should we be offering?

- What process should be used to assist clients grow their business and improve profitability?

- Can all our team members deliver these services, and more importantly should they be delivering these services?

- How long will it take to build the capability to deliver advisory services?

- How much can we leverage these services? What can be scaled?

- What would our clients value and where do they need assistance?

In essence, business advisory shouldn't be confused with compliance, or other types of advisory such as wealth, or preparing a business for sale. These latter are what Xero refers to as "complex advisory", and business advisory – supporting clients to improve growth, increase profits and to help people through insights, problem solving, strategy and implementation support – fits broadly into "simple advisory".

To add another angle to this discussion, Mindshop has sorted these simple advisory services by the following four factors:

- the services that can be delivered

- the skills needed to deliver these services

- the typical roles of the advisors delivering them

- and the tools to help an advisor in the delivery process.

When we sort by paying special attention to the services delivered and the team member skills needed to deliver them, we find that the whole spectrum of business or simple advisory falls into five "phases", which increase in value to the customer as they increase in complexity, and the capability required for your firm to deliver them.

These phases are not intended to be a prescriptive journey where all firms have to deliver services in each phase. Some firms will decide that they are best suited to phase one or two and will only focus there, while others will evolve their capabilities to deliver the more complex, but highly valuable offerings outlined in phase five. There is no right or wrong; just what suits an individual practice, its goals, target customer needs, vision and business ambitions, and the people working in it.

PHASE ONE: DATA

Any team member with basic business acumen can provide valuable facts and figures to a client about their business and industry. Information can be gathered from client financials, client questionnaires, simple discussions about the business, diagnostic tools and sharing independent papers and reports.

PHASE TWO: INSIGHTS

A deeper understanding of the data and information gathered in phase one can generate valuable information for a client. A 'rising star' in your firm is an ideal candidate to deliver services in this phase, a person who is inquisitive about business, has a moderate level of business acumen, and is confident having challenging client conversations. Business performance dashboards, 'what-if' analysis and surveys can be used to reveal these insights highlighting the 'levers' to pull in a business to drive successful change. Valuable discussions about these insights can follow on a monthly, quarterly or annual basis.

PHASE THREE: PROBLEM SOLVING

Advisors with problem solving skills can guide and advise on minor issues or opportunities impacting a business, adding significant value for the client and monetising an area that is often provided to clients at no cost. Skills and attributes required for problem solving include the ability to control a meeting effectively, a high level of business acumen, ability to structure conversations with specific business tools that lead to action, and confidence in holding challenging conversations. These problem solving meetings take the insights learnt at Phase 2 and transform them into practical strategies and actions that a client can adopt as to how to address them back in their business.

PHASE FOUR: STRATEGY

A strategic senior advisor with good facilitation skills, a high level of proficiency in strategic planning processes, and who is open to change, will be able to deliver strategic planning services to clients. Strategic advisors can tackle major issues or opportunities in specific issue-focused workshops or strategic planning sessions to provide focus, strategies and clear actions to drive a business forward.

PHASE FIVE: IMPLEMENTATION

Ongoing guidance and support for the successful implementation of strategies within an organisation requires the superior skills of an experienced facilitator able to address complex issues, and who is unconsciously competent in a broad range of business tools and processes. Advisors displaying high capability, energy and agility can deliver business advisory service offerings such as monthly or quarterly implementation support, project team implementation, in-depth coaching with the CEO or team members and annual support programs for the business.

IMPLICATIONS FOR FIRM STRUCTURE AND STRATEGY

When you break business advisory into these five phases, it becomes clear that the skills and attributes needed for success – and client value – at each phase are very different.

As you move further up through the phases many things increase, such as the:

- capabilities required to successfully deliver the service

- time required to learn the capabilities and be competent

- chargeable fees

- customer value

- impact these capabilities will have on that advisor driving the success of the entire firm

However, as you move up the phases, a few things also decrease such as:

- the ability to leverage or scale the service

- the percentage of team members with the acumen, desire or experience to deliver them

When a practice or practitioner is considering what advisory services to offer, you need to consider the following questions:

1. What phases does your firm want to deliver services in?

2. What is your current capability in each of these phases? Where are your gaps?

3. Who within the firm should be delivering the services at each phase that you want to operate in?

4. What is the ideal future position of the firm in these phases which will allow us to continue to attract and retain the right calibre of customers and team members?

No matter in which business advisory phase you're focused, there is no shortcut to success. An advisor's best clients typically gained their success over many years of continuous improvement, listening to best practice, and hard work, so why would that be any different to building success in business advisory? As customers, industry and technology innovation moves faster, advisors will need to keep pace.

In the words of Mindshop's founder Dr. Chris Mason, "If you think your education is finished, you're finished.'

Good luck on your business advisory journey.

PHASES OF BUSINESS LIFE	EXAMPLE SERVICE OFFERINGS		WHO DELIVERS EACH SERVICE & CAPABILITIES
1. DATA Facts and figures provided about business and industry trends	• Questionaires • Discussions on facts and figures • Diagnostic tools • Sharing industry papers and reports		**ANY TEAM MEMBER** • Basic business acumen
2. INSIGHTS Insights, research and analysis relating to data on the business or industry	• Business performance dashboards • Cash flow management • 'What if' analysis • Challenging client conversations • Data interpretation		**RISING STAR** • Inquisitive about business • Moderate business acumen • Confident in challenging client conversations
3. PROBLEM SOLVING Guidance and advice relating to a specific minor business issue or opportunity	• Client 'problem solving' meetings to address any issues or opportunity arising from insights • Light touch coaching & mentoring of customers		**PROBLEM SOLVING ADVISOR** • Controls a meeting effectively • High business acumen • Uses array of problem solving tools
4. STRATEGY Developing strategies for a business, specific major issue or opportunity via workshops	• Strategic planning workshops • Developing One Page Plans • Workshops on various topics such as Growth, Profit, Leadership, Change, People		**STRATEGIC SENIOR ADVISOR** • Good facilitation skills • High capability in strategic planning • Open to change & a self-starter acumen
5. IMPLEMENTATION On-going guidance for the successful implementation of stratagies within an organisation	• Annual support programs • Quarterly implementation support • Monthly implementation support • Project team implementation • In-depth coaching & mentoring meetings to address any issues or opportunity		**EXPERIENCED FACILITATOR** • Ability to address complex issues • Unconsciously competent with broad range of business tools & processes

VALUE TO CUSTOMER

CAPABILITY REQUIRED TO DELIVER

04

BUILDING THE CONFIDENCE TO DO ADVISORY

How Shaye Thyer champions change at BDO Australia

Australia is one of the most advanced accounting markets in the world. The early penetration of cloud accounting, combined with a relatively modernised and forward-thinking tax authority, has created an environment where many practices have been on the cloud for a long time and are already looking to branch out further into advisory opportunities. The industry is growing, and clients are thrilled with the new services and technologies on offer from their trusted advisors.

Larger firms have not always shared in this bounty, though. Size creates inertia, and inertia makes change difficult. When a large object is already rolling in a direction, it can be very difficult to change direction, much less turn on a dime.

This problem is especially prevalent for practices in the tier immediately below the Big Four. They're very big, and very complicated, with all of the change management difficulties that this implies. One such practice is international accounting giant BDO, where Shaye Thyer has the crucial job of National Cloud and Advisory Specialist for Australia. Recently named one of the top 50 most influential women in accounting, Shaye is spearheading BDO's move to cloud.

In Australia, all of BDO's offices are independently owned, in a federated structure. This, Shaye says, makes it incredibly challenging to deliver change on a national scale.

"What we have been able to achieve, even in a short period of time, is a sense of integration, of coming together around what we call the 20-20 vision. It's a very deliberate strategy to diversity our fee base into advisory – while maintaining relationships with our current set of clients that we deliver compliance to, with the knowledge that compliance is devaluing every minute, like for everyone else in the industry," Shaye says.

However, rapid progress is being made, and now 50 percent of all BDO's Australian clients are cloud-enabled. We spoke to Shaye about the mindset and the right moves that make rapid transformation and change possible in organisations both large and small.

CLOUD EQUALS ADVISORY

Many traditional accountants see the delivery of advisory services as intrinsically difficult because it seems entirely dependent on what are usually called "soft" skills. This often leaves accountants – accustomed as they are to concrete deliverables and keeping tight controls on variables and outcomes – unsure of how to quantify their new services, or sell them to clients. How do you approach a client and tell them that you'd like to give them some advice? Accountants who find themselves imagining this scenario understandably find themselves cringing. Why would a client want that? Is it really just talking to people?

Of course it isn't, Shaye says. Talking to people is vital, but so is technology. These two factors are bound up together, to the point where advisory doesn't just start with the cloud. **Advisory is the cloud**.

Shaye sees the cloud as so intrinsic to offering modern advisory services that they're not actually separable.

"When you put a client on the cloud, you're identifying a need," Shaye says. "You're never going to be able to select a tool that's correct for the client if you don't have some kind of understanding of the business, and that comes from an advisory conversation. So, when you put someone on cloud accounting software, you're already doing advisory."

The very foundation of advisory services always starts with the cloud, Shaye says. If the entry level of advisory services is having a "super sexy set of data" and the ability to visualise it with the client in a way that makes sense to them, the cloud underpins all of that interaction.

"You can't do that unless you have cloud. You can't do it unless the data's clean. We've got the cloud, plus clean data from our bookkeeping hub. Those things have to go together. That's the start, right?"

Having accurate, reliable cloud data is what then gives accountants the foot in the door to become advisors. It means they can start conversations with clients that are genuine, and meaningful.

"You're not just ringing clients up and saying, 'Hey, do you want me to do some advisory stuff?'" Shaye laughs. "You can actually say, 'Hey, your debtors are really high. What's going on here?'"

This, she says, is cloud – and advisory – 101.

"You need access to data to be proactive," Shaye says. "That's really key and, as accountants, we forget that all the time. As an industry, we under-leverage our access to that data. Our first step as advisors should be to properly leverage that. That's why I say cloud and advisory are intertwined."

WHY IS CLOUD A PREREQUISITE FOR MODERN ADVISORY?

[The idea that the action of putting clients on to the cloud is, in itself, an advisory service, might sound controversial, but when it's broken down, it's just common sense. Here's why.

Advisory services and management accounting require up-to-date, accurate data. But the action of providing clients with up-to-date, accessible data is also, in itself, a form of advisory. In the past, this sort of data would have required a team of management accountants to assemble. Now, it's as simple as a client looking at their Xero dashboard. Being able to see a snapshot of cashflow, debtors, creditors, invoices, and everything else that goes into the financial side of running a business puts cloud clients at a huge advantage over those who can only extrapolate financial information from delayed data in desktop accounting software or spreadsheets, which they've usually had to input themselves. And that's a best-case non-cloud scenario. Many small businesses only get an idea of where they're at during tax time, and often this knowledge is coupled with a nasty surprise from the tax department.

If an accountant is the advisor who's recommended cloud accounting to a previously desktop-bound client, that in itself is an incredibly powerful advisory action. And even if a client has discovered cloud software themselves, once they've had a taste of the power of up-to-date finances, they'll want more. It's their accountant that they'll look to, as someone who can explain what they're seeing, and who can help them plan for the future.

Of course, putting a client on the cloud is not the be-all and end-all of advisory. There's a whole world of advisory actions that follow cloud accounting adoption. But the knowledge that cloud equals advisory can help accountants who've previously wondered if advisory services are something they could ever offer.

Shaye has a story she likes to tell about how the simple act of putting a client on cloud accounting can impact their business, and act as the first step in an ongoing advisory relationship.

"My favourite story is teeny in terms of scale, but pretty big in terms of impact. It was around the first time that I learned about cloud accounting," she says.

My favourite story from that time was this little plumbing business. He's just one guy, one van, and he's got his plumbing business and he's got a wife and a little baby, and his accounts were an absolute dog's breakfast.

It was classic, you know – a glove box full of receipts and working six days a week, spending the seventh day doing his books, and he never has any cash because his customers don't pay him because he doesn't invoice them for a month, and everything was on paper.

We sorted him out and put him onto the cloud and worked through some process stuff with him – just the basic stuff. "Here's Xero. Here's Receipt Bank. Get rid of all your paper. Invoice while you're on the job. Why don't you even take payment while you're there?" All this sort of stuff. We moved right through the whole spectrum. Got rid of all of these debtors. All this sort of stuff. He actually got to the point where he dropped back to five days. He dropped his Mondays. He went, "I don't have to work Mondays. We make enough money. We're all good."

The most profound thing to come out of that, and this is why it's my favourite story, was what was actually happening behind the scenes. His wife was actually really, really unhappy because they just had this little baby, and she never saw her husband, Dad never hangs out with baby, he's always really stressed. All these types of issues. They were really unhappy, but I just remember her turnaround. His was obviously pretty profound, 'cause he was obviously happier and his business was improving and they made a lot more money and supported the family, but the impact on her was massive because she got her husband back. Dad was home now. Dad was home now on Sundays, and even Mondays as well, and wasn't fussing about with the books and all this other stuff. That, to me, even though it might have been the teeniest client ever, just, that's one of my favourite stories.

Accountants aren't psychologists, but you could see this guy was at his wits end. He was just knackered. It didn't make sense that he was struggling to make ends meet. He had a very solid business, a really great reputation, just couldn't get the actual cash in his bank account because of his process, and nobody had picked that up before. Afterwards, he and his wife said things that a lot of clients say. "I can't believe I didn't do this before. Why didn't someone else tell me about this?" "Why haven't I seen this before? Why hasn't somebody told me? Why hasn't someone saved me?" That kind of thing.

———

YOU'RE (PROBABLY) ALREADY DOING ADVISORY, EVEN IF YOU DON'T KNOW IT.

Many compliance tasks bleed into the realm of simple advisory effortlessly enough that many accountants don't realise they've been doing advisory all along. They might not have been being paid for it, or it may not have been counted as chargeable hours, but it's still advisory.

"I've been teasing out the fact that a lot of our compliance-focused team members at BDO – the majority of our staff membership – have been doing advisory for a long time. They've been doing compliance advisory, which sounds daft, but it's group restructures, it's tax planning. It's all that stuff," Shaye says.

Staff who have been performing compliance advisory tasks for years often don't recognise it as advisory, and have not yet realised that this job is in fact a useful and, when leveraged correctly by firms, extremely in-demand and profitable line of work.

"They just need to be convinced that they are capable, and maybe give them some structure to help go to the next level," Shaye says.

WHY HIDING BEHIND YOUR EXPERTISE IS DANGEROUS

Accountants tend to be experts in their field. That's one of the reasons that they are trusted advisors. A general public that overwhelmingly lacks financial expertise recognises it when it sees it.

However, expertise comes with its own drawbacks in times of widespread change. Those who are justifiably confident in a particular specialty may find themselves with a corresponding lack of confidence when that specialty becomes less relevant. For many compliance-expert accountants, the situation feels analogous to when car engine carburettors began to be replaced at scale by fuel injection systems. An entire industry of carburettor repair experts disappeared, almost overnight, because their speciality was no longer relevant, and their expertise had trapped them into a narrow area of experience, where change was feared rather than welcomed.

"There's a huge confidence issue, throughout all levels of accounting practice," Shaye says. "For partners the thought of doing something where they're not an absolute guru, is terrifying. They've always run an accounting practice a particular way, and it's this way. Moving into something different, it's hard to be brave enough to pioneer it, particularly at our scale. If you're an accountant that would seem pretty risky."

The solution, Shaye suggests, is to remind accountants that although they may feel like they're only expert in areas of accounting that are becoming increasingly automated and commoditised, their powers of financial analysis actually extend far beyond their comfort zone.

"I think we could do a lot more to bump up the confidence of our guys, to say, 'Do you know what? You probably don't appreciate how much more you know than your client who is a business owner.' Clients are not going into business because they're good at running a business," Shaye says.

For accountants, the confidence boost from the knowledge that accounting is more relevant than ever can be augmented by coaching and mentoring in the areas where they lack experience.

"I suppose our challenge from a quality perspective is going, "Okay, how does an accountant that's grown up in a traditional practice, that's probably barely touched or seen a client, actually have a more developed skill set than a business owner that's been in business for a number of years?" If our team members don't have any of that, where do they actually get this commercial skill set from?"

"I think that's where mentoring is massive, and having a culture of debriefing after client meetings. 'We just went into a meeting. You might have just sat there and looked pretty, but tell me what you thought. Tell me what you learned. What do you think we can do?' You're creating a solution at the same time as you're learning. I think there's a huge amount of value in that."

THE UPCOMING ADVISOR SHORTAGE – AND ENORMOUS BUSINESS OPPORTUNITY

Shaye maintains that the global accounting market is already suffering from a shortage of advisors, given the ever-increasing demand for these services. There has been enormous growth in both the number and scope of small businesses, all of whom can benefit from financial advice, and as the barriers to business entry come down, this trend will only increase.

"In Australia there's been such an explosion in small business. We know this thing, right? There's also an increasing preference towards locally grown, locally sold, local everything. Stuff like the coffee shop on the corner. We will see a massive bonanza of that."

Shaye predicts the shortage will get worse before it gets better, as universities and professional accounting bodies around the world struggle to match their course output to the needs of the market, creating a skills gap – but this will also create an enormous opportunity for fast-moving advisors and practices.

"All businesses can benefit from advisory services."

Shaye says that the more prevalent advisory services become in the market, the more obvious the value is to the wider business community. Practices that make the effort to create and market tailored business advisory services can expect to reap the dividends of a new boom in services.

"There's not doubt that a coach/mentor/partner/concierge, whatever it is, someone that can actually help you with those things you don't quite get, the accounting stuff that you have to do, and making sure your business makes enough money to feed your family and all that sort of stuff, is hugely valuable. Massively valuable," Shaye says.

Without this input, business owners are "just faffing about with it. Trying it all out themselves. I think there's huge value in not reinventing the wheel and actually engaging with someone that's going to prevent you from doing that. You don't have to try it all out. Someone else has already done that and someone knows about it. Let's tap into that."

Good financial guidance, Shaye says, is nothing less than a shortcut to happiness for your clients, and yourself.

Shaye Thyer, BDO

Nice to meet you, Shaye! How did you get your start in accounting?

I started as an undergrad in a mid-tier firm. I actually started a law degree straight out of uni because I always wanted to be a lawyer. I was a die-hard for The Good Wife and Law and Order, and even Ally McBeal. I started a double degree in law and commerce, and I was really, really bad at it. Normally, I'm not a genius by any means. I have to work really hard to get good marks, but that had worked well for me throughout school. If I tried hard I did all right. I tried really hard to be a lawyer, and I really sucked at it. The universe was telling me that I was not supposed to be a lawyer.

I was doing really well with all my business and my strategic subjects, so I thought, "Why not just keep doing that?" So I did, and got picked up as an undergrad at one of the local Adelaide mid-tier firms probably one of the bigger ones in Adelaide, and started very traditionally, as we do, putting collations of annual compliance paperwork together, doing tax returns for individuals, all this sort of stuff.

I think it wasn't too far in to doing those kind of activities that I started wondering: what am I even doing here? My dad has run his own business since I was a baby, so I grew up in a small business family. It doesn't make me an expert at it by any means, but I'm certainly aware of the goings on of a small business. At my first job, I always wondered, okay, we're working with clients, right, cool. When am I going to see one in real life and when am I actually going to learn how to help them, because I don't feel like these forms that I'm filling out are actually helping anyone. I get what they do. I know it's important to tell the ATO we're doing the right thing and to pay our tax, but, for me, I wasn't getting a lot out of that.

I was already a bit toey to get on to the next thing. I moved into the Finance Manager role in that firm and was in that role for the better part of eight or nine years. I guess that was my first sort of taste of running a business, albeit an accounting firm. It was really great environment for me to learn in, and I certainly learned a lot about WIP and a lot about debtors and a lot about chargeable hours and all that sort of stuff.

All that classic accounting stuff.

It didn't really make sense. I was twenty-something, and my job was to produce things for the board to gain insights and then I start to try to provide advice to them and I feel like, "You guys are FCA's. You've been around the block a bunch of times. I'm just a junior. I'm never going to tell you guys what you should be doing because I don't know more than you. You guys know a lot more than me." I think that was the first time that I started to think there's got to be a better way to do these activities.

We had this finance team of seven people, and it just didn't make sense. I look at it now and think, "Oh, my gosh. That's ridiculous." We had data all over the place. We had those big D-ring folders and all the tabs with all the management reports in it, and they were all labelled; and it took us the better part of the month to get the last month's reports out. I'd think, "That's actually really dumb." I was thinking there's got to be a better way to do this, but I didn't know what it was of course.

After I finished in that role, I went into commerce. I had the same kind of inkling, but I was still learning a lot. I'd had experience in one business. I wanted to sort of understand more about business in general, get into those positions where I actually had some skills that maybe someone else in the business didn't, that were seen as valuable, and then that would allow me to be in a position to give some people some advice and actually move the business forward.

I did that for a couple of years and then jumped into small business consulting, which is probably one of my favourite jobs, to be honest, because I think the impact of what I was doing was so close to clients. Literally everything that I did and said and helped with these clients had some kind of positive effect on their whole life, which is what I'm all about these days, now that I'm a grown up.

How did you get the role as the National Cloud and Advisory specialist at BDO?

I just did a tidy up job on the Adelaide office's finance [back] office. I won't tell you what it looked like, before, but now it looks pretty cool – all cloud. We had significant savings in terms of the business case, huge ongoing savings in terms of headcount and staff costs and things like that, very scalable.

Tell us a bit about what you like about your role in promoting the cloud at BDO

What keeps me doing what I'm doing is hearing the stories. The impact that we're having. We have a huge reach in our business here, a huge reach into so many businesses, so many lives. [It goes to show that] if your staff are engaged in things that they are emotionally attached to, and they're working with clients that they connect with on a values level, or in an industry that they're passionate about, they will do better work. When they're doing better work, the clients are getting a better outcome every single time.

How can that pro-advisory attitude gain traction in the industry?

I think that it's circular. If we're sharing the impact stories from the clients' perspective, internally, that generates more of this emotional connection with the work within the staff membership and then it's ongoing. Staff are going to

do a better job at this, and then we get more stories, and then I do
a better job.

So telling the story of how advisory works for clients is important?

Yeah. It's not clinical. It's not – you know, "if you do 1900 chargeable hours you will get X." All that stuff is so clinical. It's almost like a departure from that sort of clinical, controlled environment, to one that's a little bit softer. It's a little bit fluffier, whatever you want to call it, but it's incredibly valuable and it's holistically better. It's just nicer to be in an environment like that. Everyone feels good about the thing that they're doing. And you don't have to worry about staff retention because people are choosing to be there.

How have things changed for BDO since you brought in this focus on cloud and advisory?

What we have been able to achieve, even in a short period of time, is a sense of integration, of coming together around what we call the 20-20 vision. It's a very deliberate strategy to diversity our fee base into advisory – while maintaining relationships with our current set of clients that we deliver compliance to, with the knowledge that compliance is devaluing every minute, like for everyone else in the industry.

So over the course of this year, we've increased our cloud adoption for our clients by over 10 percentage points. We're now short of 50 percent cloud-enabled, which is great. That's been a massive win.

We've started as well to centralize some of our services, so that's been a really successful model in our UK business – making sure you're integrating bookkeeping and things like that which is really important. You want clean data. You can't advise on crap data, so you need to have clean data to actually be efficient in your compliance work and also to leverage those advisor opportunities properly.

You've talked about the importance of training and mentoring staff, either new or experienced, in advisory. Can you expand on how you do that?

One of the things that we are really keen to broaden, particularly for our more junior staff who traditionally would never have seen a client, let alone know of one existing for a number of years, is what the BDO New Zealand team calls to Two to a Tackle. [The idea is that] you never go to a meeting on your own – and that is like the simplest thing you can do to teach a junior from this stuff. There's so much value in watching and learning. We've been trying to be really clever in the way we set that up. We love to play on that we've got some big egos around the place like many firms do. Let's play on that and say, "You know what, these junior guys want to watch you. They want to watch you in action because you're awesome" – and then try and distract them from the fact that there's going to be time on the clock that they won't be able to bill, which of course is the biggest barrier, which is stupid, but it's a thing.

BDO's a big organisation by any standards. How have you managed to take your successes and replicate them across the organisation?

One of the things we try and get out is, [when something is successful] what were the steps – literally, what did you do? What buttons did you push? I think when accountants read stuff like that, from somewhere they didn't expect, they go, "Yeah, I could do that."

I don't know why, but I think sometimes we have this perception of accountants, that's probably because we are trusted advisors and top of our game and all that sort of stuff, that we're quite sophisticated learners. We're not. Accountants want to be spoon fed. They want their hands held. That is obviously really challenging to scale - but if you can do that spoon-feeding, then they go and make it their own.

And how have you made that sort of thing work at scale at BDO?

It's called BDO Drive. Three pillars: Information, intelligence and insights, underpinned by cloud. Cloud is always in there. It's a tiered advisory approach. Information is about getting the data right, getting the data clean. Basic things. Cloud enablement. Intelligence is when we start talking about things like reporting. It might be management reporting. It might be cash flow forecasting. Insights is your bucket of things like outsourced / virtual CFOs, mentoring, coaching, working through strategic things together, advisory boards, that sort of thing.

[To run that, we have our] BDO Drive champions. They're all at varying stages of their development, but they might have some particular product specialization. They might be a Xero champion or, they might be a Receipt Bank champion, or whatever it is, and they have a bunch of clients that they are, say, the outsourced CFO for. Of course, it's not like we've never done these services before. They just haven't been as prevalent as we'd like – so now we try to box them up a little bit and show people how to get started. That's been the best thing in launching BDO Drive. It's just put some structure around it, and I think accountants love structure.

You've set up advisory champions in the practice that can help others make the change. What's your advice to firms who want to do something similar?

What's definitely worked for us is that, although I'm not someone that's got a day job doing client work, I'm not so far removed that I don't "get it". You need someone who's actually still working with clients, who's tasked with pushing this thing forward. That's the very first thing – particularly in national mid tiers – if you don't have that, then you're not going to get anything done.

The other thing, that one person can't do it all. There needs to be enablement of champions in the local office. I'm a firm believer that change management is an exercise in puppetry. It's not the job of the change manager to be the face of change. It's to enable other people to be the face of change in their relevant office, or whatever it is – enabling those people with the skills, the tools, the walk, the talk, the motivation, all that stuff, to get off the chargeable hours' leash, to be able to *enable* their local teams and inspire them and lead by example.

Shaye Thyer, BDO Australia

The big lessons: Cloud equals advisory, and you're probably already doing it

Many practices still see getting their clients on the cloud as a revolutionary action, while others are doing it purely to make compliance more efficient. Pacesetters are doing it to power advisory services. The point is: no matter your reasons for putting a client on the cloud, it's a powerful advisory action in and of itself.

"When you put a client on the cloud, you're identifying a need. You're never going to be able to select a tool that's correct for the client if you don't have some kind of understanding of the business, and that comes from an advisory conversation. So, when you put someone on cloud accounting software, you're already doing advisory."

FOCUS QUESTIONS & ACTION ITEMS

Think about your most time-poor clients, those who have the most trouble with accounting and bookkeeping. How much time could these clients save if you put them on the cloud? How much easier would their lives be?

- One story that stood out to us in the BDO case study was the story of the plumber who got his life back when Shaye switched him to cloud accounting. What stood out the most to you?

- Unless you're already an accomplished cloud provider with 100 percent of clients on online accounting, your practice probably has clients who could benefit immensely from the cloud. It's time to find them!

- **Take action: If you're brand new to the cloud**, brainstorm who in your client base would benefit most from cloud accounting, plus those who are the most tech-savvy and will be most receptive to it. These are your first cloud clients. Once they've been using online accounting for some time, follow the next step.

- **If you've already got some, or even all, clients on the cloud**, ask them what the experience was like. Look for the best stories. These are great to use to sell the benefits to existing or new clients. Look also for bad stories; for those that had a bad migration or onboarding, or who are feeling frustrated. This will show you what you need to fix. Identify common themes, and use this to improve processes and experiences for new clients.

What actions are you or your staff taking that fit the definition of advisory services – whether or not you're currently being paid for it?

Even the most compliance-focused firms are often performing some advisory work. It's time to figure out exactly what that is.

Take action: There are a few ways to identify the advisory work you're already doing. Ask yourself, or your staff, to write down the most common questions that customers ask them. Meet and brainstorm what jobs are slipping through the cracks, or what advice gets given away for free in ad-hoc conversations. If you bill by time, try to identify tasks that aren't charged. Ask too what your staff are interested in; what areas of their practice they feel like they're most knowledgeable about, and what they wish clients knew.

05

PRACTICE WHAT YOU PREACH

Jason Andrew, SmartBooks Online

The importance of profitability – and empathy

For the majority of my career as a chartered accountant, I was an employee of a large firm. I spent over a decade in the boardrooms of many different kinds of businesses, advising on mergers and acquisitions, cash flow and financial strategy.

My favourite clients weren't the ones that generated the most fees, nor the ones that paid on time (as an employee, that wasn't my problem!). No, my favourite clients were the ones that listened to our advice – and better yet, implemented it. When we advised them not to use their business as a personal bank account, they did as we suggested. When we advised them of risks identified in financial due diligence, they took them into consideration in the transaction. I felt proud of the work we did. It gave me purpose.

Of course, there were the clients that didn't listen to our advice. There were some who considered our advice to be nothing more than a box-ticking exercise, to satisfy internal governance. There were others who didn't even do the basics, like regularly reviewing their financial position, or keeping their books up to date. These were – and are – often considered 'non-critical'. In the eyes of our clients, that may have been true. Founders and CEOs are usually busy, working on other parts of their business.

However, in my eyes, I felt they were neglecting what was important, at least to my worldview. I thought they were irrational, and sometimes even stupid, for not taking our advice, or even getting the basics done.

My ego raged.

To be honest, a big part of starting my own accounting and advisory business was a reactionary response to my time advising businesses. I figured, if an irrational CEO can build a multimillion-dollar company with what I considered to be minimal financial and commercial acumen, surely I could do it too, right?

I thought I was smarter than everyone else.

So I made the leap to being a business owner, and suddenly saw things from the lens of my clients. I, too, became an irrational business owner.

A MEAL OF HUMBLE PIE

When I jumped into my first business, SmartBooks Online, I thought everything would change for the better.

That was a false notion. I quickly realised I had no idea what I was doing.

Okay, I knew how to do the technical work, but I had no idea of what it truly meant to run a business. And it was costing me a lot of money.

I cringed every time I looked at my monthly P&L. Although my business was rapidly growing, we were losing money. And it didn't stop there.

Our service wasn't great, and customers were churning. As a result, I was losing more customers than I was winning. My financial and mental health was suffering as a result.

I was slaving away – 14 hours a day, 7 days a week, feeling overwhelmed and too busy to realise what I was doing wrong.

I mean, it could have been okay if I was profitable, but the truth was that I wasn't. From a revenue perspective, I was crushing it. My business was consistently doing 20 percent month-on-month revenue growth (which is impressive growth for any business, irrespective of industry or size). The problem, however, was while the top-line revenue was growing, I was actually losing money. I was servicing unprofitable customers. I hadn't designed a process on how to service our customers consistently, and profitably.

I was stuck in a profit-losing machine of my own design, relentlessly spinning wheels.

I was trapped.

PUTTING ON MY 'CEO HAT'

With the business spiralling out of control, something had to change. My business partner and I made the decision to spend a Sunday afternoon to take time away from the business and objectively analyse it. To put on our "CEO hat" and assess the overall financial performance of our company.

What we unearthed validated our gut feelings and assumptions: our business was a disaster.

The irony was that while we were supposed to be helping our customers with their firm's financial performance, I couldn't even do it myself.

"How ironic," I thought to myself. I felt like an imposter. But after a while I snapped out of it, my rational brain got to work, and we got started on addressing the problem with a customer profitability analysis.

In our analysis, we discovered that the profit generated by the top 20 percent of our customers absorbed the losses of the bottom 80 percent!

In other words, we were suffering because we were not selective about our ideal customers.

Being a 'yes' person was killing my business. It's very possible that it's killing yours too.

THE KEY TO CLIENT EMPATHY

Today, I find it ironic that, before I started my own business, I spent so much time in the boardrooms of large companies (and the garages of startups) advising them on financial strategy. The reality is that, as an employee, I lacked the empathy to understand the challenges of being a business owner. A lot of the "advice" I gave was fluff – over-engineered jargon to justify my old firm's big fees.

It was only after I began to practice what I preached that I realised what actually works. Using my own business to test financial tactics and strategies has helped me refine the advice I give to clients, and trust the process.

I also learned a big lesson in the process. It's about empathy.

Empathy is often perceived, by some business people, as a term that has no place in business. The connotations are often around being soft, emotional, touchy-feely. As something of a type-A personality (and an accountant!) I understand this perception well.

But, as an accountant that works exclusively with entrepreneurs, I need to be able to understand my clients. They're often legacy-building, creative, impulsive, busy people.

Often, accountants see things differently to our clients. We're typically logical, risk-mitigating, rational thinkers. But it's these qualities that make accountants the perfect partner to entrepreneurs and small business owners. It's our role to support our clients by adding rationality to their decisions. Rather than making decisions based on an emotional whim or 'gut feel', the numbers can augment the decision-making process, shining light on truths.

Our role is to deliver the truth. The numbers don't lie. We try to show our clients what they're saying.

But the challenge with being human is that we all have our own version of the truth.

We only have to look at the "glass half full" analogy to understand the various ways people can interpret facts differently.

Practising empathy can help us see the world through our client's lens. It helps us to communicate our version of the truth in a way that's meaningful to the user, not you! ***"Seek first to understand, then to be understood." – Stephen Covey.***

It's often challenging for us to see the world through our client's lens. To understand why they do what they do. We're quick to label them as stupid or irrational because they did not listen to the advice that would have produced a better financial outcome.

Nowadays, when a client, or anyone, for that matter makes a decision that is contrary to my views, I try harder to understand why, and to ask myself, *what would I do in this situation?*

Instead of, as in days past, pulling my hair out and mentally criticising the client for being stupid, I find myself taking the time to transport myself into their world. To understand why they did, or more commonly, *did not* make what I consider to be the obvious choice.

If you can understand how and where your clients are coming from, only then can you build the trust to show them how you see the situation, and to communicate your ideas, data, and advice in a way that they can engage with.

A complete understanding of someone's view is the necessary first step to helping them change. Practising empathy can help us be better advisors.

The ability to empathise and connect at a human level is what separates advisors from bean counters.

Which one are you?

AN EMPATHETIC PROFITABILITY ANALYSIS

Profitability and empathy aren't words that naturally go together. But, counter-intuitive as it is, considering these seem opposites as two sides of the same coin can really help your practice. When we stop to consider how our clients feel, and where they're coming from, it makes it easier to advise your clients – and select clients who are better for you, and for your business. By pairing basic questions like: "Are the client and I aligned in our values and mission? And is the client profitable?" it becomes possible to determine the true value of your clients, both in holistic and monetary terms.

Here's a step-by-step guide of how Smartbooks Online used these principles to undertake a customer analysis.

Step 1: Export a sales report

Export a sales report from your accounting system to a spreadsheet. Filter this data by customer name and rank by dollar value of sales, for the last 12-month period.

Step 2: Ask yourself some questions

For each customer, ask yourself the following questions.

1. Are they easy to work with?

2. Do they pay their bills on time?

3. Are they a brand ambassador/influencer for what you sell?

4. Do I like them as people?

For questions 1, 2 and 3, assign a score out 0 to 3 (0 being terrible, 3 being amazing). For the fourth and final question, make it binary. It's a 0 or 1. Tally your results, which will give you a qualitative score out of 10 for each customer.

Here's an example:

Qualitative Criteria	Score
Are they easy to work with?	2
Do they pay their bills on time?	3
Are they a brand ambassador/influencer?	1
Do you like them as people?	0
Total	6/10

The process of allocating a score against each question helps you to assess your customers objectively. This quantification serves to eliminate any biases you have to your customers.

Step 3: Calculate the direct cost

Calculate the average direct cost to service each customer and enter the value in a new column. You can allocate this off your timesheet data, if you track time in your practice.

Step 4: Calculate the gross profit

Calculate the gross profit earned on each customer by deducting the average costs to service each customer from the sales dollars.

Step 5: Sort your customers by gross profit

Filter the spreadsheet by gross profit of each customer and rank them per Step 2. The result is a list of your most profitable, desirable customers. They're the ones you want to clone.

And, at the bottom of the list, are the ones you may want to cull.

CUSTOMER	TOTAL SALES	CUSTOMER SCORE	COST TO SERVICE	GROSS PROFIT PER CLIENT
Tezla	£10,000	6	£35,000	£25,000
Hoolio	£15,000	4	£40,000	£25,000
① Pied Piper	£40,000	4	£55,000	£15,000
Facelook	£12,500	4	£17,000	£4,500
Tencents	£12,500	4	£17,000	£4,500
Orange Inc	£36,000	2	£40,000	£4,000
② Sassy	£225,000	8	£228,000	£3,000
Berk Hazway	£42,000	5	£40,000	£2,000
③ Purple cow	£40,000	5	£35,000	£5,000
Giggle	£400,000	8	£283,000	£117,000
Amazing	£317,000	6	£100,000	£217,000
④ Macrosoft	£350,000	7	£60,000	£290,000
Herizone	£900,000	9	£400,000	£500,000
Total	£2,400.000		£1,350,000	£1,050.000

The table above is a sample customer profitability analysis for a fictitious company, Voltage Media.

Here are the key observations.

1. The customers under 'Note 1' are the ones the owner should sack. They both rank low on the qualitative 'customer score', and they are loss-making.

2. The customer "Sassy" under Note 2 is not so obvious. They bring in a lot of revenue, and have a high customer score. However, they're being serviced unprofitably. In these situations, dig deeper to understand why this client is unprofitable. Perhaps it's because you're over-servicing them or not producing their work efficiently?

3. The customers under Note 3 are fence-sitters. They rank in the middle from a customer perspective, and they generate a small profit to the owner's business. The owner is okay to hang on to these customers, but monitor them.

4. Note 4: These customers rank highly on the customer score, and they bring in the most profit to the business. Notice how the profit generated from these clients carry the losses of the bottom half? These are the clients you want to clone.

HOW TO FIRE YOUR CLIENTS

In the 24 hours that followed our customer analysis, I made several simple, but emotionally difficult decisions that literally changed my business. I took steps to fire the unprofitable 80% of my customers.

My outreach email was something like this:

Subject: Price Changes

Hey Customer,

I'm reaching out to inform you of a few internal changes at our company. We've spent the last 12 months servicing our customers of all shapes and sizes, from startups to larger businesses. To date, we've been flexible to cater for all these different businesses as we want to help as many businesses as possible. As you can appreciate, being tailored for everyone does come at a cost. After reviewing our service offering and the associated fees, we are changing our prices. Your account will fall into the new package at £XX per month. This investment will ensure we're able to continue to maintain our level of service. Please reach out if you have any thoughts on the above.

If I don't hear from you in the next 10 days we'll assume you're comfortable with the new arrangement.

As expected, a handful of customers have left us, and were happy to accept our referral recommendation to another service provider.

What we didn't expect was that the majority of customers accepted the price increases, and continue to be our customers today.

The net result was that we actually increased revenue because the price increase offset the client loss! Making the decision to cull these bad customers built a new platform capable of efficient and sustainable longer-term growth. Although we had fewer customers, we were more profitable at a gross profit level, we had more time, we were better aligned with our customers and, most importantly, we were less stressed.

06

AMERICAN ADVISORY

Jason Ackerman of BNA CPA on the importance of talking to your clients.

For accountants, the US is a unique market with many intricacies and challenges. It's one of the most complex tax environments in the world, with almost 10,000 separate sales tax jurisdictions and a plethora of differing personal and corporate tax rules at the state and federal level.

In an environment like this, tax compliance understandably rules the roost when it comes to accounting service models. Most US firms find tax compliance and audit more than a full-time job.

Yet US businesses are increasingly demanding more of their advisors than just compliance. In the 2014 'What SMBs Want' report from the Sleeter Group, the number one reason SMBs cited for leaving their accountant was that their "former CPA didn't give proactive advice, only reactive service". Other studies and Xero's own research bears out this finding, both in the US and around the world – SMBs are beginning to see more value in advice. And among CPAs, offering advisory services are increasingly seen as not just a way to retain customers, but to attract new ones.

We spoke to Jason Ackerman at BNA CPA in South Carolina about the advisory trend in the US, how they structure their advisory offering, and what CPAs who are looking to start offering (or to offer more) advisory services can do to get going.

CLIENTS DON'T CARE ABOUT THE NUMBERS; THEY CARE ABOUT WHAT THE NUMBERS MEAN

It's important to remember that small businesses get started because they have a passion for something – and it's not normally numbers.

"There's three things that the client wants," says Jason. "The first two are: they want to save as much money as possible on taxes, and they want to not go to jail."

Because of the ever-increasing complexity of compliance, for many years, CPAs in the US have focused on these two things, in the form of tax compliance and audit work. This has mostly come at the expense of advisory, which is typically an added or tacked-on service that is probably offered ad-hoc and may not even be charged for.

But BNA CPA sees this situation as an opportunity, because **advice is the thing that clients want most**. BNA CPA sees advisory as a natural extension of compliance and tax work. It's about accepting that clients want their accountants to look not just at the past, but the present and the future as well.

"For clients, how do we make sure they're making the right decisions, that they're paying the least amount of tax possible – and on the financial planning side, that they're meeting the financial goals that they have in their life," Jason says.

"Clients like construction. They want to have a food truck. They like being a lawyer. Probably none of them have finance backgrounds," Jason says. "They want to do what they are passionate about. And it's not accounting."

This is the fundamental difference between accountants and clients. Accountants care about the numbers, and sometimes they can't understand why the client doesn't. But what they need to understand is that while the clients may find the numbers themselves confusing, they care enormously about what the numbers *mean* for their business.

"We get pretty involved with our clients," Jason says. "They're calling us all the time, asking us advice on things from – 'should I fire or hire somebody? Am I doing *too* well? Do I need to make less money? Do I need to buy things?' For a normal business, they just want to know if they're doing well. They want to know what they can improve on, and they want to know that their CPA is looking out for them."

The *meaning* of numbers is the area in which an involved CPA can make a difference, with structured, regular advisory services. It also helps differentiate your practice from others that offer only a compliance or audit focus. As multiple accounting industry reports show, clients are far more likely to leave firms that do not offer proactive advice – but, of course, that means they're also more likely to then join with a firm that does.

"I had a new client ask me yesterday: 'How are you different?' I said, 'Well, we want you to come in, we want the client communication. That's the big thing. We want you to ask questions and we want you to talk with us,'" Jason says.

VALUE THE RIGHT VALUES

One of the most important things to understand at this point is how clients value your work versus how a CPA might see it.

The key point is this: that clients care far more about the current state and future of their business (advice) than they do about the past (compliance).

There is an apocryphal story about Pablo Picasso that has him being recognised in a restaurant. A member of the public supposedly approached the famously tetchy artist, asking him if he could commission a piece of work, for which the patron would pay £100,000. Here's how the rest of the story appears in *Creating the Vital Organisation*.

Picasso took a charcoal pencil from his pocket made a rapid sketch of a goat. It took only a few strokes, yet was unmistakably a Picasso. The man reached out for the napkin, but Picasso did not hand it over. "You owe me £100,000," he said.

The man was outraged. "£100,000? Why? That took you no more than 30 seconds to draw!"

Picasso crumpled up the napkin and stuffed it into his jacket pocket. "You are wrong," he said, dismissing the man. "It took me 40 years."

The relevance of this story to CPAs is that, because many professionals have become accustomed to charging by the hour, they often assume their work is only as valuable as the amount of time they put into it. You can't turn around a job too quickly, the thinking goes, or the client won't realise how valuable it is. (The same thing often applies to staff and bosses!) This is often a hidden, psychologically-driven reason for inflating the amount of time a given piece of work takes.

PERCEPTION: How professionals *think* clients feel

REALITY: How clients *actually* feel

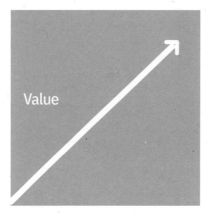

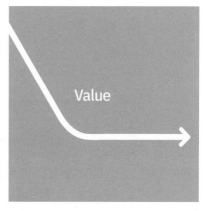

Many professionals fall into the trap of thinking that the client values how much time has been spent on a task. In reality, the perception of value has more to do with the expertise of the person or people doing the job - and for impersonal jobs like compliance, the client wants the job done quickly.

Like the napkin story, the point for CPAs is that the value offered by your service is deeper than the time it takes (or doesn't take) to complete the task. But *unlike* the napkin story, *clients know the value of your expertise*. When it comes to compliance, all the client wants is for it to be done (assuming, of course, that it's done well). For the vast majority of small businesses, compliance is a necessary chore. It's like taking an unpleasant medicine; if it's got to be done, it's best to get it over with quickly.

Advice, on the other hand, is something that businesses inherently want to spend time on. A client who understands the value of the advisory relationship doesn't want to quickly get it over with; they want to spend a good amount of time on it, and to have your expertise available to them, so they can be sure they're getting the right picture from those tricky numbers.

The key takeaway? Automate the stuff clients don't care about spending time on, so you can spend less time on it too. Take the time saved, and spend it on the stuff they *do* care about.

Put another way: Clients want you to spend *less* time on the impersonal (compliance, the numbers themselves) and *more* time on the personal (advice, what the numbers actually mean).

Here's Jason on the value of this approach at BNA CPA.

"Our team members focus on what's important, which is getting the work done. That's what really matters. We focus on velocity. We want to get our stuff done as quickly as possible because that's what the client wants. The client doesn't want the typical situation at a CPA – dropping off their documents to get their tax return done, only to have to wait three weeks. They don't like that."

FIRMS NEED TO VALUE CLIENT INTERACTION, BECAUSE INTERACTION IS WHAT CLIENTS VALUE

A key value that all pacesetting advisory practices have in common is that **client interaction is encouraged**.

"We want the client interaction. I don't understand why CPA firms are trying to get away from that, because that's how we provide our value. You want clients contacting you and asking you questions," Jason says.

At this juncture, many firms raise the following objections. One: that unstructured or ad-hoc client interaction runs contrary to (either actual or imagined) firm efficiency. Two: client interactions either add to the client's costs, or to the firm's.

These are excellent points. The fact is that, as we digitize, our lives are becoming more interrupted, which has quantifiable flow-on effects for efficiency and even happiness. This truth is often not far from most people's minds. Add client requests and questions to the already troublesome load of interruption that comes of being a connected, digital citizen, and it's easy to understand objections to ideas of being "always on." How will anyone get any work done?

CREATE A STRUCTURE FOR CLIENT INTERACTION AND BUILD IT INTO YOUR PRICING PLAN

Pacesetting practices allow for client interaction. This doesn't mean that client interaction is unstructured, though – quite the opposite. They quantify the costs and benefits upfront, and build it into their pricing plans. Successful advisory firms have found way to allow for spontaneous communication while increasing efficiency.

"If the client can't contact you, you're becoming a commodity, and they're going to go someplace else. And that's the exact opposite of what we want. Customer service is the most important thing. The whole point we're here is provide advice and value to clients," Jason maintains.

At many pacesetting firms, there are service tiers that clients can purchase, which incorporate greater or lesser levels of client access to the CPA. BNA CPA has Gold, Silver and Bronze service tiers, each of which has a number of meetings baked in. Client communication itself is unlimited. The client can call any time. These costs are estimated upfront and built into the pricing. If the scope of a given client's needs turns out to be greater than initially allowed for, they can always be re-priced.

"We reprice every year, and we have scope changes in the agreement." Jason says.

"So if the scope is the same, and I just misinterpret it, we're not going to charge them more [that year]. But that very rarely happens. When it does, I say 'Hey, we undervalued, we're going to go up next year.' But if the client wants changes, you have to say if the scope's changing. If the client asks you to do something different, that wasn't in the original scope of the engagement, you have to say 'Hey, I'm happy to do that, and this what the price is going to be for it.'"

CPAS &
ADVISORS

October 2018

Client Clientele, Inc
1234 Client St,
Fort Mill, SC

Dear Client,

We are privileged to work with you and appreciate the opportunity to review your accounting and tax needs for the coming year. As in prior years, our firm embraces a price-in-advance model for the services we offer our clients.

Once you decide upon the level of service that would best benefit you, please authorize and return the agreement to us. This document will become your new Fixed Price Agreement, defining the services we will perform for you as well as your responsibilities under this agreement.

Please note that should you require additional services throughout the year that are not included in the level of service you choose we would be happy to assist you with these services for an additional price to be agreed upon before those services are performed.

We look forward to helping you achieve your personal and business goals for the upcoming year.

Sincerely,

BNA CPAs & Advisors

An example of BNA CPA's pricing advice for clients. Note that pricing plans for different service levels are fixed, but extra work that requires re-scoping incurs an agreed-upon cost before the work is begun.

 **CPAS & ADVISORS**

SERVICES INCLUDED	PLATINUM	GOLD	BRONZE
Tax Returns			
Preparation of 2018 Not-for-Profit Federal and State(s) income tax returns, including E-filing if eligible. Includes yearly reconciliation.	•	•	•
1099 & Personal Property Tax			
Preparation of 1099s and personal property tax returns, if required. Help with setting up accounting system (Xero) one-time fee of $1,500.	•	•	•
Yearly Meeting			
Yearly meetings for strategic and income tax planning.	•	•	•
Response to Tax Notices			
No additional charge for response to tax notices for tax returns which we have prepared	•	•	
Monthly Management Reports & Sales Tax			
Monthly reconciliation of accounting software with monthly management reports and preparation of sales tax filings	•	•	
Quarterly Meetings			
Up to 2 additional quarterly meetings for strategic and income tax planning	•	•	
IRS Representation			
Representation for IRS or State audits that occur during the FPA contract year, for tax returns we have prepared.	•		
	$1,400 / month	$700 / month	$2,000 / year

WWW.BNACPA.COM

ADVISORY DOESN'T HAVE TO BE COMPLICATED

Some stereotypes are more true than others, and it's definitely true that many CPAs were brought up, or taught, to be conservative in their approach to their work. While this is entirely understandable – and it's as important as ever that numbers are as correct as possible – change is needed in order to effectively facilitate advisory relationships.

That's because advisory deals with the future, and unlike the much more certain realm of the past, dealing with the future involves making predictions. It requires a CPA to step out of their comfort zone and deal in uncertainty. The best way to do this effectively? With honesty, and based on a solid foundation of prior data.

"You can't be scared to tell the client how you actually feel, and what you think. And you can't be scared to make a mistake, because most mistakes can be fixed! It's not like brain surgery where if you make the wrong move, somebody dies," Jason says. "It's okay to make mistakes. That's how people – clients and advisors – learn."

This lesson is so important at BNA CPA that it's drummed into new staff from the moment they start on the job. Experience, including mistake-making, is necessary to be a good advisor.

"That's what we tell our young staff. You're not going to be able to start on day one giving clients advice. It takes a couple of years to feel comfortable – to know what you're doing, to be able to see problems. It's one thing to be able to do a tax return or an audit, but once you get good at that, you have to be able to see how things can be improved."

GET YOUR STAFF IN FRONT OF CLIENTS FROM DAY ONE

For a firm to be effective in advisory, the staff who are or want to be involved in advisory work have to be comfortable with both uncertainty *and* talking to clients. It's something that many accountants assume is innate; that only a particular type of person can do. Not so, says Jason; it's something that can be both taught and learned. For firms where the trend has been for years to keep clients at arm's length, it's vital to start embracing client contact.

"The way we do it is, the first couple of years you're here, you're learning under somebody, learning how to do compliance *really* well," Jason says. So far, so normal. "But also, from the day they start, they're talking with clients, and they're meeting with clients."

This is where BNA CPA diverges sharply from standard accounting practice. Many firms baulk at the idea of letting untrained staff speak to clients, Frequently, this distinction is reserved for partners and senior staff. But advisory firms are firmly bucking this trend, by removing some of the divisions between staff, but still ensuring that everyone is well-trained and knows what they need to do.

"Everyone in the firm is an accountant or a CPA, and that's their job. My office is the same as everybody else's office here. People don't start out as associates. If I'm bringing someone with me to meet a client, I don't introduce them as 'this is the associate,' I'll say, 'this is my team member who's helping on this engagement.' In that sense we're all equal," Jason maintains.

Jason goes on to say that this flat team structure enables the entire team, including new hires, to feel like they are doing a meaningful job; having a say in the firm as well as helping clients.

"There's so much a new hire can bring. A way of thinking. Someone who's been in accounting for 10 years, we might have forgotten how stupid some of the things we do are. Just getting another perspective is really helpful. We want anybody to be able to speak up and say, 'Hey, why are you doing this? What's going on?'"

Hire, or train, your people to be good with people, and staff will be able to perform the most basic, foundational part of advisory services right from the start: having conversations with people.

It's the most important first step to advisory, Jason says.

"The first thing that a firm can do is meet with their clients. Just talk with them. They're going to have all these questions, especially if you normally do stuff by email and have them at arm's length."

TAKE OPPORTUNITIES TO MEET WITH YOUR CLIENTS

Every client that an accounting firm has will have natural "touch points" – times when their numbers are first and foremost in their mind. For many, this will be around tax return time. Clients will be in the office, or primed to receive a phone call, video meeting, or a visit from their accountant. Times like this are the perfect opportunity for a firm with an advisory focus to reach out.

BNA CPA uses tax return time as a touch point. As many clients come into the office for their returns, BNA will complete the return while they're present, and use this as an opportunity to have a meeting where the client can ask them questions. It's the stuff that advisory relationships are built upon.

"We prepare the return while they're here," Jason says, "but if you don't want to do that, at least meet with them for 20 minutes, go over the information they're bringing to you, and then ask them how they're doing. They'll probably say, 'Hey, I'm thinking about doing this, and that and whatever.' There you go."

THE LAST WORD:

Jason is adamant that the most important, and most valuable, thing that an accountant can do is talk to their clients. It's the best way to give them the benefit of their experience, to build relationships, to give meaningful advice that will change their businesses and to retain clients. He notes that back in the day, before compliance reached today's unprecedented levels of complexity, accounting used to involve more talking.

"Go back to talking, just talk with your clients. Just start the dialogue," Jason advises. "That's the easiest way to start with advisory."

"I hear all the time from clients who say, 'Yeah, my old accountant, he was fine, he did the tax return, but I never heard from him the rest of the year.' If you just talk with your clients and ask them what they want, I guarantee you, they're going to say 'I *want* this. I want you to help me manage my business. I want help to save money on taxes. I want advice.' That's what clients want."

Q&A with Jason Ackerman

"I always said I was never going to be a CPA."

Jason Ackerman never wanted to be an accountant. He deliberately avoided finance when he studied at NYU – "Everyone in there was a bunch of assholes," – but then he found himself graduating at an "interesting" time. It was 2009, and the effects of the Global Financial Crisis were in full swing.

"So, I was like, I'll become a CPA, because it's a great designation and can lead you not just to public accounting, like I do now, but other things," Jason says.

After working at KPMG for three years, Jason's father persuaded him to work at BNA CPA, a practice he'd set up in 1977. "And I've been here for six years. Today might be my anniversary."

So you never wanted to be a CPA – but here you are!

The fun thing about doing advising and being a CPA these days is there's so many cool new products happening and changing all the time, that there's always something new to play with – and it's exciting. It's a fun time to be a CPA. There's no way I'd be a CPA if it was thirty years ago and everything was being done by paper and by hand. It's like, no way.

Value pricing is something that's talked about a lot in the industry, but a lot of firms struggle with it. Tell us about how it works for you.

It's an art and a skill. It takes time to learn how to do. I do most of it [at BNA CPA] and it's taken me a long time to figure out. Basically, I look at what the client needs, and then I think about what type of value am I going to provide to them, and put a dollar figure on it. I try to stay away from time, how long it's going to take. Though it can be a factor, if I know something's just going to be very time consuming, I will factor that in, but I try not to put that in because that's not what the client is asking for. They're looking for a solution and we need to price that solution according to the value they're getting.

But it is difficult. We do a three-tier pricing system for most of our clients. Bronze, gold, platinum. Bronze being the minimum, gold being the middle and platinum being more services.

How do you know if you're making money on a client?

It's pretty easy. You know if you under-price a client, pretty much right away. It works the same way if you're doing time-based billing. You know if you're going to lose money on that client, if you have to write them up or write them down. And most of the time in accounting – especially audits, or tax work – you're probably really doing value based pricing already. You're probably looking at what you charged them last year and moving it up a little bit. No matter how much time you're spending.

Audits are very commoditised now, so if you're bidding for an audit it's like you're value pricing already. For advisory services, you just have to learn. Think about a similar client and price them accordingly. But there's no right or wrong, and you could always be making more money off a client.

Tell us about how you onboard customers with a value pricing approach.

It's a lot of up-front time, especially for bigger engagement. We always look at the previous year's tax return even if it's a brand new client, and we look at the accounting system to see what's going on. When you look at the accounting system, you'll be able to tell a.) how many transactions they have, and b.) if it's a complete mess, you can start figuring out the improvements. It's pretty easy once you've done it a few times.

Can those steps be monetised?

There are firms in the US that have a 1,500 dollar client checkup. So you charge the client fifteen hundred dollars, you look at their files, see if their accounts reconcile and match their bank accounts, and while you're doing that you're analysing the client yourself to see what you need to charge to do additional work.

We don't charge for that. We look at their stuff, see if it's a mess – and then we really just listen to them, and we can hear what they're looking for.

And sometimes they might not know exactly what they're looking for but they're saying, "Hey, I need help," so we figure out what that help means and whether it makes sense for them to hire us.

You just have to have an honest conversation with them. If it's a brand new client where they can't afford your services, and you don't want to do the services for free or for cheap, you have to say, "Hey, you're not ready for us yet. But we can still help you do the tax return."

What can the accounting industry, particularly in the US, do differently, or better?

One thing? Oh, God. There are a lot of things that need to be done. I think in a broader sense, it's just providing better client service. And that means you're responsive to the client, and you help the client. And a lot of CPAs are going the exact opposite way. Which is, "How can we have less client interaction, how can we streamline all of our processes so they're so compliance driven that clients can drop off their stuff, it goes in our machine, and then it pops out a tax return we never talk to them."

I think that's the exact opposite of where you need to go.

Why is that, do you think?

I think that they think it's more efficient that way. And it's not. It doesn't help the client. I mean, we average three days turnaround from when the client comes in, it goes to review process, gets assembled, that's three days. That's way faster than normal – the average, I think, is between 16 and 21 days, for a typical firm to do a tax return. So we're more efficient – but we're still meeting with them and helping the client. If they're even just a basic client, we're meeting with them once a year. They're getting that hour of our time for advisory work.

What do your clients say about that approach?

I had someone yesterday ask me, a new client, "How are you different?" I said, well, we want you to come in, we want the client communication. That's the big thing. We want you to ask questions and we want you to talk with us. That's what we want.

Other firms are saying, "I want to become more efficient, so I'm not dealing with clients." And turning yourself into a commodity, or your firm into a commodity is not a smart way to approach the future. Because you're never gonna beat a TurboTax, as a small firm. A TurboTax will always do the return faster and better than a human, as a commodity.

It's like the old days of the industrial revolution – as if people thought they could compete with factories by hiring dozens of seamstresses and sewing really really fast.

Yeah. If you're turning yourself into a tax return factory, you're going to lose. Turn yourself into advisory.

Jason Ackerman, BNA CPA

The big lessons: Just talk to your clients. They don't care about numbers - they care about what numbers mean.

"Go back to talking, just talk with your clients. Just start the dialogue. That's the easiest way to start with advisory. I hear all the time from clients who say, 'Yeah, my old accountant, he was fine, he did the tax return, but I never heard from him the rest of the year.' If you just talk with your clients and ask them what they want, I guarantee you, they're going to say, 'I want this. I want you to help me manage my business. I want help to save money on taxes. I want advice.' That's what clients want."

FOCUS QUESTIONS AND ACTION ITEMS

Am I talking to my clients often enough, or in a way that they feel like they're getting good value for money?

- BNA CPA encourages its clients to contact them anytime, about anything. While to many accountants this will sound like the stuff of nightmares, it's been the opposite of a disaster for BNA CPA; Jason claims it has made clients and staff much happier.

- **Take action:** Reach out to your clients. This doesn't have to be all of them (but it easily can be if the outreach takes the form of an email. If you do send an email, it's worth noting what clients were most motivated to reply, and what they said, as it's possible that their concerns are the tip of an iceberg).

- If you're at a large firm, you can have staff talk to your clients; if you're smaller, you can call clients yourself. Don't overthink this exercise – it can be as simple as literally picking names at random from your client list.

- Whether you contact your clients by phone, email, text or some other method, the object of the exercise – besides the simple act of reaching out – is to establish what your clients want. Are they happy with the service they're getting? What else would they want you to do? What are they having trouble with? How else can you help them?

Is the way I currently track my time getting the best outcomes for my practice?

- Time tracking is one of the most controversial topics in accounting – if you have a room full of accountants, and you want to see a spirited debate, make an innocent-seeming remark about how timesheets are either great or terrible, and watch the fireworks. Both co-authors of this book can attest to the strength of feelings on this topic. While we note a tendency for pacesetting practices to avoid time-keeping, there are notable exceptions to this trend. One clear point from all pacesetters, though, is that you shouldn't let chargeables get in the way of talking to clients.

- **Take action:** Ask yourself, and your staff, if timesheets are right for you. Staff may feel like this is a loaded question, so it might pay to offer the ability to submit responses anonymously. If opinion is against timesheets, it may be time to look into practice management solutions that take some of the pain out of timesheets by integrating with the cloud. Or, you could trial going timesheet-free, perhaps for a limited time or for a small part of the business.

Is the way I currently bill my clients getting the best outcomes for me – and my clients?

A very common question in accounting is: should I bill by time, do bespoke value pricing, or offer a tiered payment structure? The answer, confusingly, is yes. For instance, billing by time offers both practices and clients a level of clarity and transparency around time spent, whereas payment structures offer steady cash flow. The answer depends on the needs of your clients and your practice, and where those things intersect. Evidence suggests that client opinion varies as wildly as do practice approaches. Some clients want to be billed by time, whereas others hate it. Some clients do very well on a "subscription" payment plan, others can't stand it. There is no one correct answer.

- **Take action:** If you have a preference for the billing method(s) that suit your practice needs best, asking or surveying your clients to find out what works for them is a great next step. Finding out what works best for your practice and standardising can do wonders for your workflow and cashflow, and doing this will give you the opportunity to be selective.

07

EXCUSE-BUSTING COMMON OBJECTIONS TO RAMPING UP ADVISORY SERVICES

By Liz Farr, CPA and accounting industry writer

Technology is freeing up our time from tedious data entry, and this gift of time should be an incentive for accountants to do higher-value consulting work. Yet many accountants are reluctant to make the shift from compliance work to advisory work.

These are some of the most commonly-heard objections to both offering advisory services and cloud adoption. Both these things represent full paradigm shifts for the accounting industry, so resistance is natural. But, as we'll see, even the most understandable of these excuses don't really hold water.

1. "WHY DO WE HAVE TO CHANGE? CAN'T WE DO THINGS THE WAY WE'VE ALWAYS DONE THEM?"

Automation is changing the nature of work worldwide. In accounting, the same technology that's making our work easier is also making our work more of a commodity. It's hard for clients to differentiate between the work of different firms when it all looks the same to them – and, often enough, it is all the same. So in the absence of any meaningful difference, your clients will seek out providers with the lowest prices, putting downward pressure on accounting fees.

In a session at Xerocon Atlanta called *Ready for an accounting business makeover?* Mel Power (co-founder of The Revolutionary Firm) said: "Firms today have three choices: they can go big, go boutique or go broke." In this context, going big means developing a high-volume, low-cost "compliance factory" model that uses offshore labour to save costs. Going boutique means choosing a niche for your practice and owning it.

No matter where you are in the world, maintaining the status quo will only become more difficult. For example, the recent tax reform in the US means that fewer individuals will need the help of an accountant to prepare their tax returns because fewer will be itemizing their deductions. And with many free or low-cost options out there for tax return preparation, if all you're providing is a tax return, it will be harder for your clients to justify spending £800 or more for something your staff – or your client – can now crank out in less than an hour.

Maybe you'll still do the work, but for a smaller fee? Of course, this means you'd have to do more work to earn the same revenue. Or, you could use that same compliance work as the foundation for advisory services. At Xerocon Atlanta, Keri Gohman, President of Xero Americas, pointed out that firms providing simple and complex advisory services are seeing their revenues grow by an average of 29.2 percent over the prior year.

In the 2014 "What SMBs Want" report from the Sleeter group, "*my former CPA didn't give proactive advice, only reactive service,*" is the number one reason small businesses cited for leaving their former accountant. And in Xero's 2018 survey of 1,500 UK small businesses, the top three reasons for leaving their accountant were given as "limited industry knowledge", "rarely proactive with help" and "behind on technology". Many business owners feel frustration that their accountant didn't offer additional help during the recession, and younger entrepreneurs expect more from their business advisors. If you don't start offering them what they want, these business owners will find advisors who are ready to actively engage and give business owners what they want.

2. "OUR CLIENTS AREN'T INTERESTED. THEY HAVEN'T ASKED US FOR THESE SERVICES."

Accountants tend to wait for their clients to ask for a service. But maybe this, or something like it, has happened to you:

A long-time client tells you at your annual meeting that they just engaged XYZ Firm because they needed a specialty service that your firm also provides. But they didn't ask you because they didn't know your firm also provides that service.

Before you think that it would never happen at your practice, it's worth noting that according to Xero's study of 1,500 UK business owners, almost 30 percent of these businesses are actively looking to leave their current accountant for someone who they think is more proactive, technically savvy, and knowledgeable of their industry.

If you're not communicating with your current clients about all the different services your firm provides, how do you expect them to know all the ways you can help them?

Many accountants aren't proactive enough to discuss the challenges their clients have — problems that may be obvious from the numbers on the tax returns and financials. Fearing that their clients will balk at additional fees for additional services, they don't offer their expertise to help these struggling business owners find solutions.

But as evidence that business owners are eager to pay for advice, just look at the business coaching industry, which has exploded in the last two decades. A recent research report by **IBISWorld** estimates this is a £10 billion industry in the US alone. Clearly, businesses are willing to pay top dollar for high-level advisory services that help them run their businesses more efficiently and effectively.

Accountants are among the most trusted of all professional advisors, and their relationships with their clients are among the most intimate of business relationships. Who better to help business owners tackle the challenges in their businesses than their accountant?

With all that money that business owners and executives are paying out, you could be leaving a fortune on the table if you don't start offering advisory services. And just because clients haven't asked you for these services, is that conclusive proof that they don't want additional help? Conversations go both ways. Try asking your clients these questions:

- What are the biggest challenges in your business today?

- What do you need help with that my firm can help you with?

You might be surprised what you find out when you ask open-ended questions such as these. By learning to ask better questions, as Paul Shrimpling discusses in his book, **The Business Growth Accountant**, you'll not only get new insights about what your clients want, but you'll also strengthen the relationship.

3. "OUR CLIENTS ALREADY COMPLAIN ABOUT OUR FEES, AND ADVISORY SOUNDS EXPENSIVE. HOW CAN WE ASK THEM TO PAY MORE?"

Your clients aren't *actually* fee sensitive. They're *value* sensitive. A tax return or a set of financials for their bank isn't something they want — those are things they have to buy. And because those things don't generally provide them with the insights and ideas they need to run their businesses better, they don't find them valuable. They're just an expensive necessity.

But when you offer advisory services that genuinely help business owners grow their businesses or help them achieve long-term financial goals, you're giving them something they want and desire: measurable business improvement. When they see those improvements to their bottom line or to their business processes, they will gladly pay you for that help.

Bain & Company spent 30 years on consumer research and identified distinct elements of value for both consumers and for business buyers. They found that these elements can be arranged in a pyramid, with lower value elements at the bottom and the most valuable elements at the peak.

For both types of buyers, traditional accounting and bookkeeping services are at the bottom of this pyramid. These bottom tier services include preparing accurate financials, saving clients time by doing their bookkeeping keeping clients out of trouble with the IRS, and doing this in a professional way at a reasonable price. These are what the public expects us to be able to do competently.

But as you move up these pyramids and provide services that inspire or are life-changing, you move up in value. Your clients will be more than happy to compensate you accordingly for those services.

4. I DON'T HAVE ALL THE ANSWERS. WHAT IF A CLIENT ASKS ME A QUESTION, AND I DON'T KNOW WHAT TO SAY?

As accountants, we're used to having all the answers, and as Geni Whitehouse of Mentor Plus pointed out in a recent podcast with cloud accounting specialist Blake Oliver, that's the biggest fear for most accountants. "The danger, and the fear for most of us in accounting is, if I show [a client] something that's off, or that needs improvement, that they come back to me and say, 'what do I do about it?' [that] I'm not going to know what to say."

Geni suggests seeking out the toolkits that some advisors are creating around various reporting tools such as Spotlight Reporting, FUTRLI or Fathom, and developing processes for your consulting services. Setting up consistent processes will help you become comfortable with the work, and help you improve on each iteration. This will help your firm avoid performing only "random acts of consulting", as Geni calls them.

Reporting technology tools can make it easy to aggregate data and produce reports for your clients. But don't stop at just passing a pretty report across the table. Take the time before your meeting to think about what information in that report will be most helpful for your client, then spend time with your client and explain different elements and what they can do to improve performance.

When you move into doing more advisory, you *won't* know all the answers. This is a difficult mindset shift for accountants, who like things to be black and white. However, your clients won't expect you to know the definitive answers to difficult problems. But they will appreciate it when you ask better questions and take an active interest in their business.

By collaborating closely with your clients, you'll be able to develop a set of options for them to choose from. You'll be more of a guide, suggesting possible options and bringing up consequences or advantages that perhaps would not otherwise have occurred to them. Those valuable insights, and the ideas that come out of it, are what they crave most of all.

Don't forget that collaboration with your staff can also help you find the best solutions to tricky problems. Involving the wider team will often give you creative ideas that never would have occurred to you on your own.

5. "WE HAVEN'T MOVED TO THE CLOUD YET. WE'RE STILL USING MANUAL PROCESSES THAT TAKE A LOT OF TIME."

High level advisory isn't just about technology. But technology enables you to access, manipulate, analyse and simplify data in ways that you can't when you're not on the cloud.

Automating processes like client accounting services and tax return preparation frees up time. With that extra time, you can work with more clients, or you can provide additional services to your existing clients. You might even spend more time with your family. It also reduces stress and tedium for your staff, and helps them spend less time on boring, repetitive tasks and more time doing interesting work.

I spent several months at a firm that was still manually keying in financial data when they prepared corporate tax returns. One afternoon, I demonstrated how easy it was to use their existing system to import data right into the tax software. They were amazed at how much time they could save with the tools they'd had access to for years.

When your client accounting is automated and in the cloud, you'll be able to offer your clients insights in real time, not months afterwards. And when your clients get those insights and suggestions in real time, they'll be able to make changes immediately, not months later, when it might be too late.

You'll also be better able to deal with the talent crunch in accounting when you can recruit remote employees. Having your systems in the cloud means you and your staff can work anywhere, anytime, using any device.

Changing work habits and processes is daunting. There will be an initial steep learning curve, but once mastered, you'll wish you'd made the shift years ago.

08

THE ADVISORY JOURNEY -

How Evans & Partners went from a compliance factory to advisory

When it comes to accountancy, the UK is a market in rapid transition. Although many practices are adopting cloud accounting, a majority of firms and clients have not yet made the change.

Preliminary results from a Xero survey of 1,500 UK small businesses reveals that only 13.9 percent of them currently utilise cloud accounting services – but it also shows that many of the over 60 percent of businesses surveyed still running on spreadsheets or desktop accounting are looking to adopt cloud in the near future.

Similarly, clients who are looking to change practices, identify a lack of advice and/or not having a cloud accounting offering as their primary reason for switching. These factors, plus the looming deadlines for game-changers like Making Tax Digital and Brexit, mean the time is ripe for forward-thinking practices to create market-leading cloud accounting and advisory services.

In uncertain times, knowing that you should be changing is one thing, and understanding how you can go about it is another. The most useful thing, for many UK accountants, is still a real-world example of how it all works in practice.

This is the story of one UK practice that went from compliance to advisory, and is now more successful than ever before – and there's plenty of advice here on how your firm can do it too.

Bristol firm Evans & Partners is a Xero platinum partner, and was a finalist for UK Accounting Partner of the Year at Xerocon London 2017. We spoke to practice principal Olly Evans about what it takes to transform a firm from old-school accounting to a world-leading, cloud-focused advisory firm.

FROM FRUSTRATION TO NEWFOUND ENTHUSIASM FOR ACCOUNTING

Olly Evans first trained as an accountant over 25 years ago, but quickly found himself frustrated. He decided instead to see the world, and built a career in management consulting. But, after 14 years, he returned home to Bristol, to work at the family business – Evans & Partners.

"It was a very compliance-orientated business – a compliance factory," says Olly. "They were really good at what they did."

The problem was, Olly goes on to say, clients weren't wanting compliance services as much as they had during the first 40 years Evans & Partners had been operating. Many clients were beginning to do basic compliance for themselves, or were wanting more from the accountant-client relationship, and Olly felt like the world was moving on from the old ways. He wanted to be able to spend more time with clients, and provide more value than the practice could manage under a paper-and-Excel system. It was time for the cloud.

"When I got back into accounting it was the same as when I left – very backward-looking and paper-based," he says. "Seven years ago, I went to a conference and I saw Glen Foster from Xero doing a demo. I thought, 'This is great, this is what I've been waiting for.' I became the champion that pushed it forward in the firm and said, 'This is how we need to do things.'"

SELLING THE CLOUD TO SCEPTICS

It wasn't easy at first. Change often isn't. But, Olly says, switching to cloud accounting and offering advisory services has paid huge dividends for Evans & Partners.

"I was working at the time with lots of people who didn't necessarily see the value in the cloud," Olly says. "So I just took the view, 'I'm going to show this to all our new clients'." Olly's role in the practice at that time was to win new business, and the cloud was just the ticket.

"I said to [our clients], 'This is the tool, it's really good for you, and really good for us.' We gradually built up the cloud practice, and it grew and grew and grew."

Much of the internal resistance towards adopting the cloud at Evans & Partners came from technical staff who saw Xero as just another software product. The way to convince the sceptics, it turns out, was to showcase client successes.

"We set up a couple of people as champions and we started training clients as well, so that helped smooth the first six months," Olly says. He made sure the firm kept stock of how easy it was to take care of their cloud clients versus their paper or spreadsheet-based customers.

"We just found that it was so much easier to service those clients, that the team actually started saying, 'This is good, this is helping us, we need to get this client onto the cloud as well', and it built and built from there," Olly says.

He says that if he could do the cloud implementation all over again, the one thing they'd change is that they'd do it faster, and more comprehensively – taking a lot of the pain out of the process.

"We're now much stricter with new clients. We say, 'We actually really want you on the cloud.' It's not that we're giving less choice, we're just saying, 'This is the better tool to do things with,' and that we can give our services to them much more effectively," Olly says. "We could have done that earlier, made it more comprehensive, and gotten more clients on the cloud faster."

HELPING OLD HANDS WITH THE TRANSITION

Olly says that the hardest part of transforming Evans & Partners from a compliance factory to advisory was taking a team of old hands into a new business environment. Many employees were technically competent and good at fixing business problems under the old model of once-a-year meetings, so the change to more client contact could be tricky.

"A lot of the staff who had just done compliance work would go in to [meetings] and talk about the accounts from nine months ago and the client really wasn't very interested in that," Olly says. Staff across the business had to change their mindsets and focus, to that of advisors who caught up with clients every month or every quarter.

"The focus is no longer on the compliance work, it's on, 'let's get this up to date, let's get it so we can understand it, let's get it so we can advise clients with it'. That's been the biggest and hardest challenge," Olly says.

The way they've met the challenge and brought the team along is through focusing on team communication. Evans & Partners have away days where they get together, talk about how they're going to tackle a particular problem, process map it out and work their way through it.

"We'll put together people that would be champions in certain things so that they can pilot it on a group of clients and refine it, work it out from there," Olly says. "Those things have all come together in the last couple of years, but [recently] it all just kind of clicked, so it's working really well."

OVER THE HUMP

Once the cloud was entrenched in the practice day-to-day, compliance became relatively effortless. It's not that they don't do any compliance at all – rather, with the time freed up by cloud efficiency, Evans & Partners were able to change the way they worked with clients.

"We're spending a lot more time actually talking to clients and listening to clients, that's the big difference," Olly says. "We'll meet with clients every three months, sit down and talk to them about what their goals, aspirations, and plans are. It means they have to down tools, we have to down tools, we sit in a room for an hour and talk about their business."

As well as their base-level services, they're developing advisory services and packages that they can easily monetise and sell as added value to clients.

"When we started working with cloud clients we realised that they didn't expect us to just engage with them once a year.

They would come to us with a lot of questions. So we're doing a lot more day-to-day support, and we're turning that into a service as well," Olly says.

"We are developing a real-time accounting service at the moment so we can manage all the data processing for [clients], which gives them peace of mind, gives them less stress, gives them the gift of time and gives us data we need to advise them on. So it's an absolute win-win."

Since the transition, the numbers have all been going the right way for Evans & Partners as well. "We're doing a lot of our work more cost-effectively. We're making better recovery on our jobs, we're not carrying so much work in progress, we're doing the jobs faster. All those good things are happening," Olly says. "We're in double figures for growth, percentage-wise."

Evans & Partners are also seeing clients come to them, simply so they can work with a cloud accountant.

"They come to us and say 'We need someone who really gets it. My other accountant just spoke to me once a year and they didn't seem to help very much,'" Olly says.

THE MARKET IS MOVING TO ADVISORY, SO MOVE QUICKLY

The market has never been more receptive to the advantages of cloud accounting, Olly says, and the future belongs to firms who embrace it. While it won't necessarily be easy, it is essential for practices that want to keep up.

"Work out your plan. Where are you trying to get to? Why are you trying to get there? What are you passionate about? Because you'll do that faster – if you've got something you really want to do and you really enjoy doing it, you'll make that happen fast," Olly says. "Work out who your champions are, work out the clients that you can convert over, and just get on with it and do it as fast as you can."

He says that for practices considering making the move to the cloud, and from compliance to advisory, the time for change is now.

"The cloud is our platform for doing business, and the market is really responding now. In the last 12 months, we're seeing a lot of new businesses coming to us wanting to work with the cloud. If I was in that position I would just want to do it as fast as I could."

Olly Evans' top four tips for managing the journey from compliance to advisory

1. Hire from industry

Olly looks for new hires in unexpected places: he specifically wants new staff who have experience in the hospitality and retail industry. Customer service experience is rapidly becoming a must-have skill for the new generation of accountants. It's no longer a student-days blip on CVs.

"We try to find people who've got some experience in hospitality or retail, and have customer experience in some form or another. They can actually talk to customers, build a relationship, and they can deal with issues if they arise. You might see people who have gone through education recently, maybe have a little bit of experience, they've had a bar job, they've worked in a store doing something, those are really good skills."

2. Make the most of up-to-date data

The ability to have up-to-date information to advise clients with is the cloud's single greatest feature. But it's only good if you use it.

"You need to sit down with somebody and say, 'This is what your business looks like, these are the margins you're making. Xero is the market leader, and the open platform, 600 add-on apps, the ability to take that central data and do things with it... We're using it to collect data from our clients – bank information, invoice information, process – and then do our reporting bit at the end."

"I had a meeting with a client recently who runs a £2 million trade business and he said, 'Look, I don't understand these numbers at all.' We went through some stuff and then he emailed me at 4 o'clock in the morning and said, "I've got it, this is it! If we do this we can take two percent off the supplier cost, we're going to make an extra £60,000." It's that kind of helping somebody

understand their business better, that's why the cloud is really good."

3. Minimise pain during the transition by working with Xero

"When you do projects you look at the benefits versus time. You always have a dip where things get harder, so the benefit is negative, and then it picks up again. You need to be aware of that – so how are you going to manage that dip, how are you going to manage the point in time when it gets a lot harder?"

"You can do that through working with the Xero partner team. They'll help you go through the process. They've got some really good education tools to show you how to work and have templates and things you can use. Get your champions set up in the business so they know the product really well. Pick what clients you're going to work with. Start with the easy ones, get those done, so you minimise the pain, you learn more and learn faster and you grow it from there."

4. Talk to other cloud practices

Working with and talking to other cloud practices has been fundamentally helpful to Evans & Partners in managing the transition from compliance to advisory.

"That's one of the really beautiful things about the whole Xero ecosystem. Partners tend to be really open, they're really happy to talk, to share ideas, and the pains that they've been through. We all pretty much share the same issues. I've been lucky to sit down with other partners and talk to them – and Xero facilitate lunches and roadshows and all sorts of things where we get a chance to talk."

"I'm always really happy to speak to other partners as well and just share what we've done and what we've learnt to help them. I don't feel like we're competing at the moment, there's such a big market."

THE EVIDENCE FOR WHY YOU SHOULD ADD ADVISORY SERVICES TO YOUR PRACTICE OFFERING

The main reason you should add advisory services, from a practice perspective, is easy to articulate: it can help the practice make more money. A lot more.

Our research suggests that UK practices who have implemented advisory services make, on average, nearly double the revenue per client of practices that only do compliance.

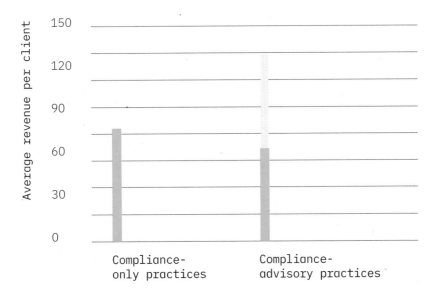

Figure. Comparison of average revenue per client for practices with and without advisory services

An interesting point to note, however, is that while advisory and compliance partners report greater overall revenue per client, compliance revenue is a lower part of the total. When we asked partners for details, they explained that there's a shift to charging clients separately for advisory services, instead of simply giving these services away to justify higher compliance billings.

As improvements in accounting software continue to make compliance easier, the value of compliance-only services across the industry will be reduced.

Practices that choose to offer advisory services on top of compliance will find that it offers more than just a stop-gap solution. We believe that much of the value of Xero and its suite of apps and add-ons is in that it makes it possible for accountants to offer up-to-the-minute advisory services for clients – **making the role of accountants in business more vital than ever.**

Advisory services, of course, mean many different things to different accountants. To break this down a bit more and help illustrate how your firm can start to think about providing advisory for the first time, or how to expand on existing services, we've extrapolated the revenue reported by participants in our benchmarking for nine different kinds of advisory service, and shown how the percentage breakdown would look for a firm with 250 clients.

Service	Share of advisory revenue	What revenue would look like for a firm with 250 clients
Advisory services, e.g., budgeting, cash flow forecasting business planning	29%	£259,000
Virtual or outsourced CFO services	16%	£143,000
Startup mentoring, advice, and networking or assistance with business development	12%	£110,000
Capital-raising/assistance moving to better interest, terms or financing options	11%	£95,000
Succession planning	10%	£92,000
App/software (other than accounting) setup, configuration and support services	7%	£65,000
Business performance benchmarking	6%	£53,000
For-fee implementations of accounting software for businesses that are unlikely to become long-term clients	5%	£40,000
HR advisory services, e.g., assistance setting employee compensation, planning to add/ reduce employees	3%	£30,000
Total		**£887.000**

Olly Evans, Evans & Partners

Olly Evans is a partner at Evans & Partners, a multi-generational practice founded by his grandfather in Bristol. Despite doing his training over 25 years ago, Olly was initially reluctant to work as an accountant, seeing it as an industry that was mired in tradition and getting left behind. Instead, he worked as a management consultant and travelled the world. Olly returned to Evans & Partners with the advent of Xero and cloud accounting, and he's since helped transform the firm from a "compliance factory" into a market-leading business advisory accountancy – while making their compliance work much more scalable and efficient. They now advise over 1,000 businesses in and around Bristol, and are the South-West's first Xero platinum partner.

Olly thinks he owes some of his success story to where it's set. "Bristol has the advantages and opportunities of any big city. It also has an intimate, friendly vibe which is perfect for any business owner. There is a flourishing community of advisors and mentors. It's resulting in substantial growth in the tech and creative industries."

As a gateway to the South West, Olly finds that connectivity contributes to the opportunity. "I regularly meet up with other Xero advisors and discuss what's working and what isn't. I meet countless business owners who have set up in London initially, but have decided to improve their lifestyle and reduce costs by relocating to Bristol."

Q&A with Olly Evans

How did you come to be the cloud champion for your firm?

I left accountancy and got back into it about 12 years ago for personal reasons. When I got back in, it was the same as when I left, very backward looking and paper-based. I went to a conference and I saw Glen Foster doing a Xero demo seven years ago and I thought, "This is great, this is what I've been waiting for." I became the champion that pushed it forward in the firm. I was working at the time with lots of people who didn't necessarily see the value in it so I just took the view, "I'm going to show this to all our new clients." It was my job to win new business so I said to everybody, 'This is the tool, it's really good for you, really good for us." We very gradually built up the cloud practice and it grew and grew and grew.

How do you find navigating the politics of that? Because there's often some resistance towards new ideas and new ways of doing things.

There was resistance, and a lot of technical staff just saw it as another software product, just like Sage. We set up a couple of people as champions and we started training clients as well, so that helped smooth the first six months because there were fewer issues, [and] it came with free training. We just found that it was so much easier to service those clients, and the team actually started saying, "This is good, this is helping us, we need to get this client onto the cloud as well," and it built and built from there. So it was organic growth to start with. It wasn't easy, it was hard work, [but] it did change.

Knowing what you know now – now that you've taken the firm through this stage – if you could go back in time and do it again, how would you do it differently?

Faster. More comprehensively. We're now much stricter with new clients and saying, "We actually really want you on the cloud," so it's not that we're giving less choice, we're just saying, "This is the better tool to do things with, we can give our services to you cost effectively." We could have done that earlier, and just made it more comprehensive, and got more clients on the cloud faster.

Just the ability to have information to advise clients with, and sitting down with somebody and saying, "This is what your business looks like, these are the margins you're making." I had a meeting with a client recently who runs a £2 million trade business and he said, "Look, I don't understand numbers at all." We went through some stuff and then he emailed me at 4 o'clock in the morning and said, "I've got it, this is it. If we do this we can take 2 percent off the supplier cost, we're going to make an extra £60,000." It's that kind of thing… helping somebody understand their business better, that's why [the cloud] is really good.

What's been the most challenging aspect of this changeover?

Taking a team who are very technically competent – very good at fixing the problem at the end of the year, so they can assimilate a lot of data and process it and fix a single point in time, from eight or nine months ago, and say 'there's your perfect answer – it's been challenging going from that to someone who has to do that every month or every quarter, so the focus is no longer on the compliance work, it's on, "let's get this up to date, let's get it so we can understand it, let's get it so we can advise clients with it." That's been the biggest and hardest challenge.

Thinking of some of those obstacles, what's the way that you've navigated around that kind of thing?

Through training. Partly through selling the services to clients – [if] we have to deliver it, we have to learn how to do it. Bringing the team along, we have away days, we get together, we talk about how we're going to go through a particular challenge or problem, then process map it out and work our way through it. We'll put together people that would be champions in certain things so that they can pilot it on a group of clients and refine it, and work it out from there.

Olly Evans, Evans & Partners

The big lessons: every firm can make the change, if the vision is clear and staff are supported along the way

It's 100 percent possible to transform a big firm from compliance to advisory – and the rewards are well worth it.

"Work out your plan. If you've got something you really want to do and you really enjoy doing it, you'll make that happen fast. Work out who your champions are, work out the clients that you can convert over, and just get on with it and do it as fast as you can."

FOCUS QUESTIONS AND ACTION ITEMS

What steps stood out to you as the most important things Evans & Partners did in their advisory journey?

- To us, setting up cloud champions and training clients stood out as an important step. What do you think was most crucial to getting it right?

- **Take action:** Identify staff who like talking to people, who are interested in technology, who want things to change for the better. And if that person is you, chances are you'll need help. Chat to the staff at your firm. Who'd be interested in a change champion role? What does success look like, and what might the rewards be?

Who in your practice is going to be most worried about, or threatened, by a move to the cloud, or greater rollout of advisory services?

- It could be partners, seniors, juniors, administrative staff. Young or old, there exist people who fear change – for what are almost always reasons that make perfect sense to them. Staff who are great at getting bank link software to talk to desktop accounting software worry that their skills no longer matter. Spreadsheet wizards fret that their preferred tool's infinite customisability and utility will no longer be wanted.

- Dealing with change in traditional industries is several books, if not a whole library, on its own, but at the most basic level, finding out about who will have the most trouble with change is an important action. These people can be nurtured through the process, and if done properly, they'll often become the change's biggest advocates.

- **Take action:** Showcase stories of client success to sceptics. This book is a good source, and as you go, there will probably be great examples among either your own clients, or among the clients of another practice whose success you wish to emulate.

What do your clients want that you can turn into a service?

Olly was surprised when he realised his cloud clients wanted to hear from their accountant. Evans & Partners found that moving clients to the cloud automatically led to more client contact and questions – so they packaged day-to-day support and other engagements into paid services. It's an important reminder that what your customers want should help determine the services that you provide. How might this apply in your practice?

Take action: Accounting practices often think they know what their clients want – but have you asked them what *they* want? It's time to leverage your client list. To do this, there are plenty of easy-to-use online survey tools like SurveyMonkey that can be sent via email or embedded on your website. For a wider view, there are also Net Promoter Score tools like AskNicely that help practices get high-level and in-depth knowledge of exactly what their clients think of their service – and help you create new services to satisfy demand.

09

EMBRACING THE CHANGE IN ACCOUNTING

By Will Farnell, Farnell Clarke

Accountancy is changing

Once we've made the choice about whether or not to become a completely digital practice, we need to ask ourselves: what does the practice look like? How bold will it be? How ambitious? What resources are available? What's the endgame?

We have two options; to do nothing, and bury our heads in the sand, or to decide on survival and adapt for it.

Billing by the hour will likely cease to be an option when the client can clearly see that the process of compliance is automated, so we need to change both our and our clients expectations. Advisory work will have to replace income that will be lost, and the success of this approach depends on us providing a better services to clients, ensuring we're responding to the changing market, and explicitly recognising that data entry and box ticking is likely to be replaced by robots.

That's why I often say, "Compliance is dead." It's not, of course – I use it to grab attention – but while compliance will never *truly* die (it will, in fact, remain fundamental to our services) the fact remains that we have to get our approach right. And for as long as we focus on selling commodities, our primary focus will be price sensitive, forced down by mostly or fully-automated and offshored compliance-only shops, and our firms may die as a result. That's why we have to change our approach. Just changing tech isn't enough in the long run. We need to develop new product or service lines to replace this revenue – and sooner rather than later. Only changing the business model will stop firms from being left behind.

Everyone tells us to be advisors, but advising what? The word means different things to different people. Most firms already call themselves advisors (without necessarily defining what they advise on – even when a client asks them!) An advisory-focused firm needs to be clear on what we're going to advise, how we propose to do it, and how to communicate this to existing and future clients. From that, we can work out whether we have the skillset to do what we're planning, and if we don't, we can investigate how to acquire it, whether this is through partnering with someone, changing equipment or tech, bringing on technologists instead of out-and-out accountants, or whatever else is most appropriate to our firm and its plans.

LOOKING BACK: A BIT OF ACCOUNTING HISTORY

Compliance only became the focus of accounting firms across the world because it got so complicated – more so in recent times than in the past. In the UK, for example, the institution of self-assessment created 31 January deadlines. Then, in 2012, RTI (Real Time Information) was introduced, and everything else that has come along since has meant almost constant change in the way compliance needs to be dealt with. It's not surprising that's what clients most cared about, and what they most needed help with.

For a long time, making sure accounts complied with the latest laws, regulations, and requirements meant that there wasn't time for very much else. Go back to before this happened, to before relationships with clients were changed by these compliance pressures, and accountants delivered more. Technology – when applied correctly – has now given us back that time, so now we have to look at how we can regain those deep-rooted relationships with clients where they can't imagine having a business without an accountant as an advisor, sounding board, and more.

The problems for firms adopting this old paradigm anew is that their underlying business model must change. How do you adopt pricing models to deal with the pressure on compliance fees, and to adopt more advisory roles? If we accept that firms need to become advisors, we need to think differently.

So if we accept all this – that compliance is being automated – we have to replace the compliance revenue. This means reversing the downwards trend that links service cost, value, and time recording, as well as wanting to bill by the hour because the tech makes the job more efficient. **It's time to accept that, when it comes to compliance, you have fewer real billable hours, and therefore less revenue**. Once you get over that mental hurdle, you can consider what you do to replace this.

DEMONSTRATING VALUE AND PRESERVING INCOME

Accountants need to think about income preservation. If we accept that charging by the hour for compliance will eventually fall by the wayside, even if time tracking itself does not, we know we're going to lose that income – and losing 80 percent of our income isn't clever. **The client gets the same value before or after automation**, so we have to look at what it is we're actually doing. And that won't be selling minutes in a day any more, but delivering an outcome – whatever that might be. It's important to note at this point that delivering that outcome to our clients faster than we used to doesn't decrease the value of our service; in fact, it's the opposite, and we need to be prepared to defend this to clients and potential clients.

As tech replaces our compliance practice, and we think about the new or expanded services we want to provide, we need to identify the skills we need to do it. Sure, tech can't replace the human factor, but if you currently only talk to your clients once a year that's not much of a human factor. We need to create more services as products, depending on client requirements, using the data we already have - but, as James Kay (Farnell Clarke's MD) says, we always need to nail core services first.

Put another way, when I'm consulting to other firms, I generally start the discussion along these lines, and ask first whether they accept that there's downwards pressure on fees. From there, we talk about how automation will drive efficiency and effectiveness in the products and services that firms have historically delivered. Once a firm accepts that, and understands that tech is going to make their work processes more effective, I ask if they accept the need to replace some of the revenue that will inevitably be lost.

THE LIGHT AT THE END OF THE TUNNEL

At this point, the obvious question is: how? How is this revenue going to be replaced? At the start, firms often don't see many options. Some already provide a full service, with private finance management divisions, wealth management, insolvency, and other services they can sell. In the past, these services have been expensive and exclusive. So I ask: what about the everyday client who wants to make sure his home business won't go bust and who needs to set up a pension? I ask what other services they're able to deliver, and whether they've considered other ways in which they can support their clients.

So what does the firm do with the freed-up time, resources and utilities? This is where there's a great opportunity: replacing the *perceived* value of compliance services, and actually delivering *real value* by using compliance and the data behind it to deliver information that kick-starts new conversations with your clients. These things are truly valuable to the client, because they genuinely help them, and this can help maintain – or increase! – fee levels.

LOOKING AGAIN AT BOOKKEEPING

It's at this stage we need to discuss bookkeeping. In the past, it's been seen by accountants to be low-value and has been left to the clients, historically using desktop software and (often) a shoebox full of receipts. That's because it wasn't cost-effective, as it wasn't easy for a practice to do without sending people out on house calls. Now, the first real value of the tech available today is to make bookkeeping a viable service line. However, it's more than just that, because when you have the bookkeeping data, and if you're updating it regularly, you're in regular contact with the client. This is where you can start building relationships; learning about the client, their objectives and aspirations, to provide value in the future.

Of course, this depends on what the bookkeepers are doing and the needs of the company. If your client is a small limited company or sole trader paying a nominal monthly fee, it's now easy to do their bookkeeping with Xero plus a pain-free app to record receipts – which means they might not need a bookkeeper at all! Bookkeepers need to realise this, and adapt their offering, examining where they can add value to the client and move beyond charging for data entry. Studies have been done around automation and the data entry roles at risk, but, as we've seen with other industries, such changes often result not in job losses, but in a change in the work that people do.

"Having data is vital. It enables us to look to the future, and to make plans to allow us to achieve our goals." – James Kay, Managing Director, Farnell Clarke

—

LET'S LOOK AT DATA

Client data is something with which we're all familiar, but the successful digital firm needs to be aware that other forms of data exist. Data from our own processes and efficiencies, from client business trends and competition, internal data, and data on how we interact with existing and future clients, partners and suppliers.

Collecting and analysing all available data is important for us, because it helps us expose variability, optimise operations, understand how best to serve our clients, and more. We need to find new ways to record such data, since examination of large amounts of client data helps uncover hidden patterns and correlations that can create competitive advantage and result in more effective marketing and communications. That, in turn, will increase revenue.

—

WHY I SET FARNELL CLARKE'S STRATEGY TO BE CUTTING-EDGE FROM THE START

Historically, accountants go to university, leave, and then join a firm on some professional form of training contract. They learn how to be accountants, qualify, and either a.) stay where they are, do really well, become a partner, and continue to drive the firm the way they were taught; or b.) they might leave the practice and go to industry, taking their skillset with them. This is a completely different environment, and they are either lost to the practice, or will set up their own practice sometime in the future. Since they'll more than likely set up their firm in the way they were taught, it's likely nothing will truly change.

Double-entry bookkeeping was devised in the 1400s, and in many respects is still exactly the same today. As a profession, we're not *that* up for change. We've used the same processes, the same structures and – when it arrived – the same software. Yes, of course it's evolved – from ledger to spreadsheet, to Sage and desktop accounting software. Now we're going through the next step, from cloud technology to a fully digital firm (for some) and from the desktop to cloud technology (for others.)

When I set up my firm in 2007, most accountants did what they had been doing for the last 10 years. I had the benefit of not having been trained in the old way, so I had no preconceptions about what my practice should look like. I was able to think through how I'd like my accounting firm to look, and from the start I wanted to have no charge for ad hoc meetings, and transparency on prices. At the time, that was pretty novel.

At the same time, the internet had arrived, and we were comfortable with it. I thought there must be accounting products that one could use online. It took about 18 months before we found a product we thought was right. To adopt it seemed like a complete no-brainer. Why wouldn't we want access to client data 24/7? Why wouldn't we want access to the same ledger on which our clients were working? Having just one version of the ledger has so many advantages. With this, it became possible to provide the type of bookkeeping services accountants have historically avoided. This gave us the opportunity to help clients process transactions, and to assist in decisions in a timely manner.

PROVIDING FOR GROWTH

I often hear about firms that aren't comfortable with the idea of taking on more clients, even if this is a direct result of needing to change to survive. For the fully digital firm, this is much less of a concern. Growth is about scalability, and scalability is about digital transformation. Above all, it's important to recognise that technology is an enabler in the widest sense of the word. It's fine to say, "Use Xero instead of Sage 50," but **the biggest challenge is that firms have to understand that their underlying business model must change**.

How to ensure you can cope with more clients

- Partner with the best

- Share knowledge and learning

- Stay open to ideas, opportunities, business models and more

- Ensure processes are seamless, transparent, and repeatable

- Keep staff updated

- Understand and map how to transition clients

- Understand how different client habits and processes hit the bottom line

- Never settle for staff who aren't quite right

- Ensure you have all the skills you need in the firm

- Constantly look for ways to improve

- Never stop recruiting – if you're on a growth curve, don't ever stop being open to finding good people

AND FINALLY

Every firm is different, with different characters and clients. There's still time to differentiate yourself, and to implement the advisory services that are going to be vital to the future of your firm. Think to the future, and about more than compliance. To implement the upcoming changes, ensure that client data is accurate, maintenance is timely and relationships are more than an annual compliance-based meeting. That means setting a strategy for development, and knowing who your clients are – and who they're not – from the start.

10

ADDING ADVISORY: A PRACTICAL PATH

With Gary Boomer, CEO, Boomer Consulting

An apocryphal, ancient Chinese curse is said to say: "May you live in interesting times." Today, accountants and bookkeepers might just agree. Right now, practices all over the world are trying to figure out if the advent of cloud accounting is a blessing or a curse. Financial and business headlines proclaim the "death of accounting" – and some companies play right along, suggesting that accountants aren't really needed any more, and that the compliance work that many practices rely on will soon be a thing of the past.

However, rumours of the death of accounting have been greatly exaggerated. While cloud accounting software has been a harbinger of many changes to accounting practice, accountants are more important than ever to the small businesses that rely on them for advice.

But how to take advantage of this change? Accountants and bookkeepers understand that offering advisory services is the way of the future. The problem is, many don't yet know how to start.

We asked Gary Boomer, CEO of Boomer Consulting and one of Accounting Today's 100 Most Influential People in Accounting, how firms can effectively introduce and build advisory services. Here's what he told us.

The three levels of accounting services: a practical advisory framework

There are three main levels of accounting services – compliance, simple advisory and complex advisory. Most firms focus on basic compliance services, but demand for these is changing. New technology continues to make these tasks more efficient, or in some cases completely automated.

Pricing for compliance services is also becoming more and more competitive, and clients have an increasingly diverse range of compliance tools to choose from.

Accountants and bookkeepers are also discovering that new technology built into cloud accounting software offers stronger analytics capabilities, giving them deeper insight into their clients' financials.

These gains in efficiency and analytic capabilities give forward-thinking accounting professionals a once-in-a-lifetime opportunity – to reinvent their profession. You can now devote your time and expertise to advising clients on the best course of action for their business.

Advisory services can distinguish your firm from the competition and let you provide more value to your clients. This equates to greater revenue and continuous, long-term engagements.

Let's start by taking a closer look at the three different levels of accounting services – and the opportunities and downsides associated with each one. Please note that although many firms start out offering just compliance, these different levels don't necessarily represent a linear journey; they're three distinct service models that build on and interact with each other.

This diagram is a basic overview of the common breadth of services. As you achieve higher levels, you're differentiating your firm from others in the crowded market. This allows you to increase profitability by providing greater value to the clients you serve.

£ COMPLIANCE	££ ADVISORY PERFORMANCE	£££ ADVISORY STRATEGIC
Tax	Business advisory	Strategic planning
Accounting services	Family office	Mergers & acquisitions
Assurance	Wealth advisory	Succession planning
Technical advisor: Hindsight-based perfection	Trusted advisor: Insight-based progress	Trusted advisor: Foresight-based progress

LEVEL ONE: COMPLIANCE

The vast majority of firms operate at this level, offering services like tax, financial reporting and bookkeeping. However, firms that are limited to this level face the prospect of diminishing revenue. Competition, the efficiencies gained through new technology, and the widespread adoption of cloud accounting, are having a big impact here.

Until the emergence of cloud computing, the primary value of level one services came from the amount of time they required. Many hours were devoted to process-driven tasks like bank reconciliation and data cleanup. Today, these tasks can be accomplished in a few minutes, since the processes can be almost completely automated by cloud accounting software.

LEVEL TWO: SIMPLE ADVISORY

At this level, accounting practices are focused on analysing the health of the businesses they serve. Services like business intelligence and growth profitability are common. This is the level where most of the big four firms operate. You will find some level one practices dabbling in simple advisory services, but often only to a limited extent.

LEVEL THREE: COMPLEX ADVISORY

Firms that offer complex advisory services are analysing performance but also advising on the best course of action for their clients. These practices help their clients with strategic planning, forming succession plans and managing risk, as well as many other tasks.

As the graphic above shows, revenue opportunities only increase as you move up the levels. The main goal is to move away from being valued solely for your time, into a role where you're valued for your financial expertise. You're striving to be seen as a trusted advisor on all your clients' financial matters.

Technical advisor versus trusted advisor

When you operate strictly at level one, you're more of a technical advisor. It's an execution role, where process-driven tasks – like tax preparation and monthly reconciliation – must be carried out 100 percent correctly.

The *trusted* advisor is more of a visionary. This role is about balancing perfection with progression. You're striving to help your clients by offering creative courses of action and solutions. You can do that through the combination of data and your expertise.

Accuracy is still crucial, but advisory services allow you to present various options to a client. Some of them will be optimal and others may not be. The trusted advisor educates the client on their different options so they feel empowered to make decisions that are best – for themselves and their business.

Many accounting professionals operating at level one claim that they just don't have the time for advisory services. These professionals are opting for minimal revenue, when so much more is within reach. Gary Boomer's exact words on this sum up the problem succinctly: "Level one professionals are too busy picking up £1 bills to bend over and pick up £100 bills."

1 Menue and services
2 The team
3 Packaging and pricing
4 Platform and ecosystem
5 Unique processess
6 Clients and filter

Is my firm prepared for levels two and three?

Firms need to be proficient in level one services before advancing into the upper levels. Many will fall somewhere between level one and level two. Such practices may offer advisory services when the opportunity arises, but they don't make them the centrepiece of their services menu.

This is a good starting point. But if you want to move completely to level two or three, you need to have a solid foundation in place. The graphic below shows all the pieces of the puzzle that must come together if you want to move into the full advisory realm.

It's often overlooked, but this transition also requires a shift in mentality and strong change management. Individualism and change resistance are classic traits of accountants and bookkeepers. It's traditionally a heads-down, methodical profession.

But advisory services require a team approach – with your internal team and also with the client. If you want to reinvent your practice and client relationships, you must be open to working in new ways and making changes.

Take action: Add advisory services at your firm

As we've seen in our case studies, firms that are successful in introducing advisory services tend to do best when they make the following changes. Many of these action items are suggested elsewhere within this guide, but we've compiled them all here to form a complete checklist for preparing to offer additional or higher levels of advisory services.

Identify the right leader and team members

You'll need people who possess specific skills – and the right person to lead the team.

Create filters in your client list

It will help you prioritise the clients that are suitable for your new services – and filter out the ones that aren't.

Develop a menu of services that covers all three levels

You should keep the services that are popular among your existing clients. But you should also introduce higher value services that can attract new business and increase revenue.

Package and price services based on value

Tiered pricing bundles clearly define the service options available to your clients. They also ensure that your practice is properly compensated.

Define the processes

Assign roles within your team and be certain that each part of a client agreement has an owner.

Build a cloud ecosystem

Collaboration is much easier with the cloud. Cloud-based document storage, financial software, project management tools, video conferencing and email can help your practice run smoothly.

Transforming your client relationships

Once you feel comfortable positioning yourself as a trusted advisor, you can begin pitching your new services to your clients. Advisory services won't make sense for all your clients. It will also take time to roll them out to the clients they do suit. By following the four steps below, you'll make the move from technical to trusted advisor and enjoy greater profitability.

Step one: Identify the right opportunities

This first step is essentially a fact-finding expedition. You'll need to talk to your clients and find out what they really need. This means asking them the right questions and listening closely to their responses.

You'll want to learn about your client's business operations. Even more importantly, you'll want to find out what their pain points are. Ask about their long-term goals, their typical day and even how much time off they're able to take. Eventually you'll find out how and where you can help them.

This is also the stage where you'll identify which clients are a good fit for advisory services – and which are not. Some clients are simply set in their ways. Some aren't receptive to outside help when it comes to the direction of their business. Others will be interested but might not be at a stage where you can offer enough help to justify the time and effort.

Step two: Transform the relationship

Once you've identified the difficulties the client is facing, let them know how you can help. Specifically, explain the benefit of working with you in an advisory capacity.

This is where the mentality shift comes into play. Accounting professionals often tell their clients "what it is" and "how it's done" but gloss over "why it's important." However, the "why" is where you explain your value. These conversations can also help you refine your advisory services over time. That's because you'll learn what works for your clients and what doesn't.

As well as explaining your own value, you'll also need to demonstrate the value of the software and other technology that drives your advisory services. Some clients might want to see the software in action and learn how it works. The majority will just want reassurance that you believe in it. Make it clear that you know the system well and are confident that it will improve your client's operations.

As you move into a new arrangement with the client, you'll need to be clear on services, pricing and ownership. Explain from the start what your responsibilities are, what the client's are, and what the cost will be. If the client deviates from those terms, don't be afraid to have the necessary conversation to get things back on track.

A good way to prevent issues from arising is by using a pricing matrix from the start. The client can let you know what services they're interested in and what they're willing to spend. You can then use the matrix to determine if their requirements are within budget. If not, you can prioritise your services with them before the engagement begins.

Step three: Become the trusted advisor

Once the relationship is established, start delivering your advisory services. It's important that you encourage your client to handle their responsibilities, and also gauge their satisfaction. A key part of keeping clients happy is being proactive. Check in with them regularly so you can prevent small issues from growing out of hand.

Decide who will be the point-of-contact for each client. A partner can usually handle these duties for a smaller firm. Bigger practices might need to assign account managers. These staff members can meet with clients frequently and gain a strong understanding of their business. They can even offer new services that might suit a specific client but not your entire client base.

Another advantage of account managers is that they possess customer service skills, which typical accounting professionals may lack. They can speak to clients in terms that make sense to them, as opposed to getting bogged down in accounting terminology.

Account managers can also respond in a way that is mutually beneficial to the client and the practice. Accounting professionals often feel pressured to come up with an immediate solution when confronted with a client's issue. Account managers, on the other hand, should be skilled in coming up with a new service offering that solves the issue in a way that is profitable for the practice.

Step four: Increase your advisory services

At this point, your firm is offering level three, complex advisory services. The key, going forward, is to refine your services and bring in more clients.

Start by analysing your own operations – just as you would for your clients. Look for opportunities to increase revenue and efficiency. Your processes will need to be continually refined. That way you can do more without immediately expanding your staff.

You'll also want to attract potential clients with your advisory services. Consider offering a 30-day trial of your services. This will help build trust and can quickly put a sceptic at ease. You should be confident in your advisory abilities at this stage. If so, it's likely that most companies accepting the trial offer will become paying clients later. Those that don't probably weren't a good fit for such services anyway.

Your new role brings new rewards

The sky's the limit once you've completed the transition into the trusted advisor role. You will be helping to shape businesses and have a direct impact on their success. And the potential for increased revenue is just too great to ignore.

11

PRACTICE MAKES PERFECT: AN ESTABLISHED FIRM TRANSFORMS FOR ADVISORY

Before becoming a thriving advisory firm, WK were already a pacesetting practice.

The Marlborough-based accountancy practice was one of the first firms in New Zealand to fully implement Xero. They were the second Xero platinum partner anywhere in the world, the first multiple partner practice to commit to Xero Workpapers and Xero Practice Manager, and they've been a Xero Partner Advisory Council member since 2012. They've had longer than most firms to enjoy the efficiencies of running entirely on the cloud.

But, not long ago, they were on their latest attempt to implement advisory services, having failed at several previous attempts. The rationale was that, if they could get back time efficiencies from their compliance work, they'd be able to invest those into advisory services with clients.

They'd first tried outsourcing business advisory services, then hiring a one-person specialist team. Neither of these steps was successful. They then tried training their entire team in specialist advisory tools and techniques. This met with more success, but there was limited opportunity and scope for some staff to implement their training on the job. Ultimately, they couldn't get the advisory cut-through they were looking for.

This is a familiar story to many firms who have implemented limited advisory services, or have even tried to roll them out at scale. Many can sense the immense potential of advisory, but they're left frustrated, with a half-baked implementation that never rises to greatness.

What, then, made things different for WK?

WK director and advisory champion Neil Sinclair says there were two main factors in the firm's successful advisory implementation. The first, and most important, was starting with a shared vision and strategy. The entire firm – the staff, the directors, and everyone in between – collaborated on a shared decision to offer more value to their clients by making advisory services part of the DNA of WK.

The second success factor was the adoption of a framework that provided the entire firm with a structure that could be used to define exactly what advisory was at WK, as well as the skills and tools necessary to do it – and, most importantly, what everyone's role in advisory was.

Neil is keen to share with other firms the story of how it worked for WK, to help them get it right first time.

"The important thing is there is no shortcut to advisory. Investment in true capability is the prerequisite," Neil says.

PART 1: PUTTING ADVICE AT THE CORE OF THE PRACTICE

When the WK directors were planning to offer business advisory services at scale, they were still missing a vital piece of the puzzle – but they didn't yet know what that was.

They'd soon find out, thanks to their own staff.

The team of directors knew they had to put advice at the core of the firm's values, and to do that, they went through a process to decide what the new values would be. "We decided that we really liked values ICE, for integrity, caring, and excellence," said WK director Hamish Morrow.

But when the directors took the values to the staff, they faced an unexpected, if low-key, revolt.

"We sent those values out to the team and the response we got back was, 'That's not WK, that's not what we are all about – that feels really cold. Are you sure you've got it right?'"

"We were a bit taken aback," Hamish says. "Staff don't normally say things like that. We said, if you think you can do better, go for it."

WK's staff did think they could do better, and they did. They came back with a new set of values: ADVICE, which added accessibility, dedication, and vibrancy to integrity, caring and excellence.

To transform your firm to deliver advisory services, everyone needs to be on board

It's easy to see an exercise in choosing new values as lip-service, or management mumbo-jumbo – and it easily can be, if it's not done sincerely and carefully. Values are only of use as long as everyone genuinely buys in, and if they're treated as foundational to the rest of the business. But because both of these things were true of WK's implementation, the results have surpassed everyone's expectations.

Hamish says that the open approach was pivotal to winning the hearts and minds of their staff. Everyone was involved in the process, everyone talked through what the firm wanted to achieve, and everyone played a part in shaping the firm's core vision, mission, and values.

"That one moment has been transformational at WK, because it has put advice at the centre of everything we do," Hamish says. "Everyone lives and breathes 'ADVICE' on a daily basis, and staff love seeing the results that we are achieving with clients.

"That was so critical. I look back on our journey, and strongly believe it was the single biggest change point in our process – actually understanding what we wanted to do as a firm and getting the team alongside us with the values. Once we had the values and the core vision and mission ingrained in everyone's DNA, it was a very simple process to take the team along with us for the journey along with us."

The next step in the journey: an advisory-focused structure

The WK team's other big revelation on their advisory journey was that they needed to have a very good understanding of what advisory meant for them, and be disciplined about sticking to it, in order to keep it at the core of their firm. To do that, they created a framework to give the often-debated notion of "advisory" solid structure and meaning.

'We've adapted a pyramid framework that Michael 'MC' Carter from Practice Paradox developed. MC's pyramid was the first time that we saw real clarity around how we could roll out advisory services at scale. It talks about the seven layers of value that an accountancy firm can provide to its clients," Neil says.

"We changed MC's pyramid a little to work for us. For example, in MC's pyramid the first layer is Real Time Data. We think this is fundamental to doing advisory well. But with having Xero data for the majority of our clients, real-time data is a given at WK. So we removed it from our pyramid, despite it being the first fundamental decision to transforming into an advisory firm," Neil states.

"Our first value layer may surprise you – we firmly believe it is compliance! You can still add a lot of advisory value into client relationships by doing compliance well. Tax planning, for example, we see as a compliance-based layer of advisory.

"Then, there are three levels of what we call financial advisory, which is about helping clients fully understand what their numbers mean, and formulating key actions they should take based upon those numbers. It's important that we present the numbers in a way that makes sense to our clients, giving them that clarity. For that, we have a suite of tools that we use to make data more meaningful and clear for clients. We use Xero report packs, and other reporting add-ons, and format data to get key messages across to the clients.

"The next levels are commentary, then accountability, which is about how we make clients accountable for the things they say they will do once we've talked with them, and the numbers have told their story. All of that is built into our financial advisory area. Then, levels six and seven of that pyramid are strategy and implementation, which is getting to the big stuff where we have highly trained specialist advisors operating.

Importantly, the pyramid also acts as a filter for matching staff skills to advisory duties. All staff can perform advisory services up to level three, and the remaining, more complex levels are tackled by staff determined by their aptitude, experience and skillset."

WK Pyramid

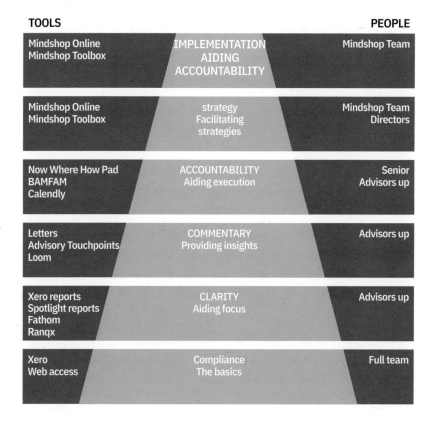

TOOLS		PEOPLE
Mindshop Online Mindshop Toolbox	IMPLEMENTATION AIDING ACCOUNTABILITY	Mindshop Team
Mindshop Online Mindshop Toolbox	strategy Facilitating strategies	Mindshop Team Directors
Now Where How Pad BAMFAM Calendly	ACCOUNTABILITY Aiding execution	Senior Advisors up
Letters Advisory Touchpoints Loom	COMMENTARY Providing insights	Advisors up
Xero reports Spotlight reports Fathom Ranqx	CLARITY Aiding focus	Advisors up
Xero Web access	Compliance The basics	Full team

The WK pyramid framework is based on the "Value Pyramid for Accountants and Business Advisors" by Matthew "MC" Carter at Practice Paradox (practiceparadox.com.au Used with permission.

Advisory touchpoints

A vital part of embedding advisory in everything WK's staff and directors do has been the creation of Advisory Touchpoints – an all-staff key performance indicator that is run and tracked out of Xero Practice Manager, WK's practice software.

The basic idea is that in every interaction WK has with a client or a client's data, there is the chance of discovering or adding something that can create value for the client.

"We are very loose with what an advisory touchpoint means," Neil says. "For some clients and cases it could be: here's a benchmark report from Ranqx. Or it could be that we recommend a Xero add-on, or show them how particular Xero files work, or suggest they do something different. All of those things are opportunities to add value, so we would class all that as an advisory touchpoint."

Because touchpoints are tracked in XPM, reports can be created to measure how the firm is performing.

"Every job we set up on XPM has some advisory touchpoint tasks, and when a staff member deals with an advisory touchpoint over the course of their job, they record time against that particular task.

"This system gives WK the ability to see a.) what percentage of jobs have had an advisory touchpoint and b.) what type of advisory touchpoint they are doing with clients. Then they can track the benefit of those advisory interactions with our clients, in terms of the actual improvement and the client's results.

"It gives us really rich and credible reporting we can say, hand on heart, we know that we are adding value," Neil says.

Achieving this KPI is directly aligned with firm success, and it's incentivised accordingly. "All of our senior staff have this KPI as part of their bonuses – they must achieve 80 percent of their annual jobs with the advisory KPIs achieved to even be *eligible* for a bonus," Neil goes on to say.

Now that he's often called upon to talk about the success of WK's advisory implementation, Neil is adamant that practices need to realise that finding a structure for their advisory services is one of the most important actions they can take.

"We've had four attempts of getting advisory going, and the first two were spectacular failures," Neil says. 'The fourth one, based on this pyramid, is a spectacular success."

A key part of this success, visualised within the pyramid structure, has been matching the advisory services that clients are wanting with staff who are qualified (or have the aptitude) to deliver them.

"In our experience, only 20 percent of your team will excel at levels 5 and 6 of the pyramid, the strategic advisory stuff," Neil maintains.

"For 80 percent of advisors, being a business advisor doesn't mean that you have got to go and help clients with leadership development programmes, or book strategic plans, or uproot their mission and values, or look at the marketing plan, all those other things. They can extend their accounting skills a little and offer real value for clients, but also have the comfort to know we have specialist advisors there to assist where the client demands advisory services at that next level. We now have two career progression ladders in WK, and staff really appreciate that."

WORKING TOGETHER: NEIL GIVES A WK CLIENT CASE STUDY

We have a client that is on level six to seven, strategic advisory, so we've done strategic planning with them. They're on a monthly reporting cycle, and they attend monthly governance meetings that I sit in on. This is a business owned by a husband and wife so they have never had governance at all before. They now do, with me and the bank manager sitting in as well, and we simply go through: Where are we now? Where do we want to get to? How are we going to get there? We pry through those. We also come up with three to four things we want the client to work on, assign them to individuals within their business, assign timeframes, and we drive the business that way.

He's been doing that process with us for two years now. He started out with a profit of about £150,000. Year one, we improved on that £150,000 to about £600,000. Year two, that improved further to £850,000.

Our fees for that particular client have gone from a fiver to £30k. So he's paying a lot more with us. After year one, he said, "Jeepers, I'm actually spending a lot of money with you guys." I thought, "Oh no, here we go." He says, "So, I used to spend five grand and I made this much, now I'm spending 30 grand and I'm making that much. That's a lot more than what I just spent with you. That's the best investment I ever made, right?"

I thought, well, that's pretty cool. I said to him, "Well, I can't take all the credit for that. You've done all the hard work. You've come up with the answers, I've only facilitated the process. The market has also changed, the market has improved. So some of that increase is because of the change in market." But he goes, "Yeah but if you hadn't taken me through the process and you hadn't allowed me to work on these elements of my business, I wouldn't have been able to take advantage of that market change. So you can't not take credit for that."

So that's a pretty cool story. If you think about Rod's vision, from the start of Xero, that's what he used to talk about all the time. It is hard to believe, when you start off on the Xero journey, that clients are all of a sudden going to pay you 10 times more than what they used to and you are actually going to get those results – but that was the vision that Rod, that's the vision that we shared, and it's why we were so early in adopting Xero. Once you fully understand how to really embed that advisory plan in to your business, in to your accountancy practice, it does allow you to make quite transformational changes for your clients – and that is very rewarding, hugely exciting.

—

THE IMPORTANCE OF ADVISORY TOUCHPOINTS

One of the most striking things about how WK do advisory at their firm is their use of advisory touchpoints in Xero Practice Manager.

The reason this stands out is that most accounting practices are split into teams, with clearly delineated and separate responsibilities. Speaking (very) broadly, at many firms teams tend to be split into number-crunchers, and people-talkers – a division that's often related to seniority.

At WK, things are different. Advisory touchpoints are a key KPI for all staff and directors. Someone whose main job is running numbers can note an interesting quirk in a client's data and filing an advisory touchpoint, as can a senior advisor who's just come off a meeting with a headline client. Because advisory is "baked into the DNA of WK," it means that all staff members are always looking out for the next opportunity or conversation starter around advising clients. And, because advisory touchpoints are set up and tracked in WK's practice management software, XPM, they're a concrete, measurable indicator of the firm's progress – rather than the fuzzy, undefined thing advisory is often seen to be.

It may seem like a simple thing, but it's one of the foundations of WK's advisory success.

—

Once the values and structure are in place, you can train and hire the right people

With the whole team on board with the new vision and values, and a structure that apportioned advisory roles and tools, WK was able to ensure that current employees were happy and that future hires would work well in the new firm paradigm.

"I reckon 20 percent of the people that come in to accountancy practices have got the ability to operate in the level five/six area, in that real high level strategic advice/innovative strategic advice area. The other 80 percent are still incredibly valuable to us, as a firm and as a profession, but you have got to channel their skills and their energies in the right way," Neil says.

"We recruit on values now, and that's a key part of it. We actually look for people that we actually think do the advisory stuff really well. That's why the pyramid I keep referring back to is so critical, in my view, in terms of making an accounting practice an advisory practice."

The operating changes at WK have led to a fully-engaged team, and staff say it's a much more rewarding place to work. Prior to making these changes, the firm used to share the common accounting struggle to attract and keep good talent – but the new reputation that's come with their new advisory focus has changed all that.

"We used to struggle to get graduates to work for us, but we now regularly have 100 or more people apply for roles. In the past, we might have five or six."

PART 2: THE RIGHT TOOLS FOR THE RIGHT JOB

A values-based transformation and a new strategic framework were the two pillars of WK's successful new advisory structure. But doing advisory wouldn't be possible at all without the right tools for the job.

The tools WK uses are separated into two categories: software and skills.

Anatomy of an advisory app stack

"Using technology well in your business or accounting practice, and developing an app stack that suits your style, is really critical," Hamish says.

WK's software stack starts with the Xero platform. The trifecta of Xero, Xero Practice Manager, and Xero Workpapers handling foundational tasks of compliance and practice management. Then there's a layer of practice software geared to maximise efficiency of client interactions, including SuiteFiles and Practice Ignition, plus Loom and Zoom for client-facing video recording and meetings. Dedicated internal communications tools include Yammer and Zoom, and the firm maintains a social media presence on the biggest networks: LinkedIn, Twitter and Facebook.

After that comes the reporting tools, including the Spotlight tool suite, Ranqx, Fathom, Excel, and others. These tools play an important role in the firm's advisory operations by enabling the quick creation of reports, benchmarking and budgeting for clients.

The fourth layer is client apps, for customers in particular niches or industry verticals. Marlborough is a wine-producing region, so wine industry apps Vintrace and Vinsight feature here, as well as Dear for inventory tracking, Figured for agriculture, and WorkflowMax for clients who require job costing.

Each app is mapped to a particular function of the WK advisory pyramid, so the use case for any app is always clear. The criteria for consideration in the stack is: does using this app add value to the client and to the practice? Hamish gives the following use case.

"Instead of writing a letter, I quite often use a Loom video now," Hamish says. "I can go on and I can see the clients are looking at that Loom video three or four times. The feedback that I get is usually, 'That was so much better than the old six page letter that I used to get.' You can actually describe things in a much better stage when you are actually talking!"

The rapid pace of change has come with a steep learning curve, but Hamish says that coming back to the question of client value – as well as asking whether a given app fits with the practice's values – can help practices understand what apps are worth investing learning time in.

"It takes a little bit of getting used to. I didn't like to see my ugly old mug on these videos when I first started, but clients really appreciate that stuff. The stack of apps you can use these days is just mind blowing. It can really add value, so constantly reviewing that app stack is really important."

It's vital not to take a scattergun approach. WK is careful not to offer or support every app, as it would quickly become impossible. Instead, they focus on apps that we think will create a critical mass in terms of what they offer for the client. They are selective, making sure that the apps they support will have a wide appeal amongst their client base, helping them achieve a better result for clients.

"We ask ourselves, is Loom going to enhance the client experience, and can we get our advisory mission through to clients better using Loom instead of other alternatives? Yes, we can. It is meeting our core vision, mission and values – so it gets selected."

Selecting a new app

The WK app stack is managed by a Senior Advisor with responsibility for our Technology Advisory Services, Jenna Gilbert. Jenna explains that the process of looking at new apps is mostly done through networking. WK engages with firms who are on a similar journey stage, and listens for app-related tips and tricks. Once identified, new apps are implemented on a case-by-case basis, depending on how simple it is to use and set up. Once there's a broad staff consensus that the app squares with the practice values and mission, WK will train two or three champions in the app's use, so that other staff have the opportunity to reach out if they need help.

For more complex apps, there's a slightly different process. An example would be Vintrace, the winery management app.

"We know it's unrealistic for all our team to know the app. So we'll select specific experts in Vintrace. We do that with all the more complex key apps that we work with – be it Mindshop, Vintrace, Figured," Jenna says.

For client-facing, complex apps, Jenna adds that it's important to treat the vendors as partners.

"We invest heavily in them and we expect them to do the same. That's really worked for us over the years, and we've developed really tight, strong relationships with all of those app vendors, so that we can tap in to expertise and knowledge within the app's company itself if we need to."

Tool	Pyramid Layer / Function	Purpose
Xero	Compliance	Annual Reporting
Xero Practice Manager	Compliance	Timesheets, billing, Tax
Xero Workpapers	Compliance / Clarity	Workpapers
SuiteFiles	Compliance	Document Management
Xero V2 Reports	Clarity	Non-annual compliance reports
Spotlight Reports	Clarity	Management Reporting
Spotlight Dashboard	Accountability	Snap Reports
Ranqx	Clarity	Benchmarking & What If Scenario planning
Fathom	Clarity	Management Reporting
Excel	Clarity – Accountability	Complex Budgeting / Analytics
Spotlight Forecasting	Accountability	Simple Budgeting
Loom	Commentary	Explanation videos for clients

Zoom	Commentary - Accountability	Online meetings with clients
Mindshop Online	Accountability - Implementation	Client planning, accountability meetings, client education
Practice Ignition	All	Client engagement
Connectworks	Compliance	Trust / Company admin
Figured	Client App	Agri reporting and budgeting
Vintrace	Client App	Winery management reporting
Vinsight	Client App	Winery inventory management
Entryless	Client App	AP automation
Dear	Client App	Inventory
WorkflowMax	Client App	Job Costing
Yammer	Communications	Internal Comms
Facebook	Communications	Social Media
Twitter	Communications	Social Media
Vimeo	Communications	Social Media
Zapier	Communications	Links comms
Arlo	Education	Education Management

The hard thing about soft skills

The other half of WK's practice toolkit is staff training and "soft skills" tools, which WK procures through Mindshop, a subscription-based learning and development solution and virtual coaching team, founded in Melbourne in 1994 by Dr Chris Mason.

Although Neil is cautious about coming off as a walking billboard for Mindshop's services, it's impossible for him to not talk about them, as he credits their advisory training, tools, coaching and systems with playing a huge role in WK's success in the advisory arena.

Jenna explains that one of the most important of these tools to WK's advisory efforts is called a "Now, Where, How," which is used in client meetings to get a snapshot of a client's current situation, where they want to be, and how they're going to get there.

"I have a little printed pad that goes with me everywhere, and on it is a very simple process. We take the client through three simple questions: where are you now? Where do you want to get to? How are we going to get there? Then we got a bit deeper on the how, and define: what key steps do you need to take? Who is going to do it? When is it going to be done by? That's important, because then the client has a plan," Jenna says. "We love Steven's Covey's 'Big Rocks theory' and are continually helping clients define and crack their big rocks."

This format is also useful for keeping the advisor on the rails, says Jenna, as accountants have an innate, human tendency to know best, and to leap straight to "now" from "how" without getting or giving any context to what is a priority to fix first. It's better to coach than to consult, he says, defining the latter as telling people how to do something, and the former as helping them come to the right understanding on their own. It's much more effective.

"Then what is even more important for us is an advisory touchpoint – it's to ring up and say, remember, a few days ago when we talked, you said you were going to do this, and how you were going to do it. How are you doing?" Jenna says.

"Doing this is actually helping clients, by reinforcing the link between what the numbers are showing, and what changes or what things they have to do to improve their business. Then helping them further, by holding them accountable."

FOURTH TIME THE CHARM

WK's successful advisory implementation means happier staff and clients

Neil rates WK's previous three attempts at implementing advisory services between 3 and 5 out of 10, and their current effort, which they branded internally as "WK Engage" as a 10 out of 10 for the practice. But he's quick to say that this is the start of a journey, not the end. There's always room to improve, to learn, to grow. His advice to other firms who are themselves early on the advisory journey, or struggling to get started, is to realise there is no shortcut. The substantial rewards of advisory are the product of good foundational work – and the way to build that foundation is to start with your staff. "The advisory tools we use are very easy, but embedding advisory into your practice is not simple. There is no shortcut to doing advisory well. You must invest in advisory capability," Neil says, emphatically.

"I keep coming back to it, that story I tell about ICE vs ADVICE. The most important thing is, having a very deep clear, understanding on what you're trying to achieve in your accountancy practice. It is critical. And it's not a surprise, right? Accountants tell clients to do that all the time. We just don't often do it ourselves," Neil says.

He says the results have been more than worth it. Advisory is profitable and sustainable, and compliance continues to feed the firm's advisory efforts.

"Because of the strategic decision that we made that we wanted to become advisors and we wanted advisory to be core and part of the DNA of WK, it hasn't necessarily always dropped to the bottom line – but has it made our clients more sticky? Has it improved the results we are helping our clients achieve? Has it improved Marlborough as a place to live?" Neil asks.

"The answer is yes to all of those questions, and that is what we are all about. That is what our strategy is all about."

Meet the Advisors: Q&A with Neil Sinclair

A lot of firms find it difficult to conceive that their staff or their old hands could actually pull this advisory thing off, because it takes a different set of skills, than, putting it bluntly, bean-counting. When it comes to advisory, can old dogs learn new tricks? If they can, how do they do it?

This old dog has learned a few new tricks along the last 12 months. I think they can, but the old dogs have got to be comfortable, to be able to change. They have to be comfortable with the fact that it will change the way that they operate. I think one of the other things that we struggled with initially, is that this advisory thing must be really difficult and really hard because it seemed nobody was doing it that well.

That's very true.

Yet, when you understand it, it's actually not that difficult. But you still have to have the right skills and mindset to operate it. You have got to be absolutely 100 percent committed to becoming an advisory firm.

The best example of this I can give you is, think of the old style accountant. You would've come to me and said, "Neil, I have got this tax issue." Right, I am going to go, "That is easy, if you do this, and this, this will get around it for you." So, I will have given you an answer.

Now, you would come to me and say, "Neil, how am I going to develop my business further, because I want to grow, because I want to take my grand-kids to Disneyland." I'm going to be, "Well let's talk about how you are going to achieve it. What are you going to do? How do you think that sales are going to work?" So you are asking a lot of questions, helping you drive down to the areas of the business you need to change to actually achieve that objective. You aren't actually giving answers.

That is a difficult process. To think that you can put one partner, or have one team that is going to do the advisory only – don't think will work. That was our first failure. Second failure was saying that everybody could do it. But where we actually got it right, was saying, look, advisory is a whole scale of things from here to here. The top end is this stuff of strategic planning, leadership development, marketing, HR and all that. But level two, three, four, for most accountancy firms – which is clarity, commentary, and accountability – is where the sweet spot is.

So, for firms that can pull it off, it is a huge point of difference, and a potential way for them to make more money.

Absolutely, there is no question – but you have got to remember the pyramid base, which is still for us the online data and the compliance side. You have got to have good efficient processes, which you build this whole thing from. For us, the platform we built this on is still Xero Practice Manager and Xero Workpapers. We couldn't have done advisory the way we have, without our processes moved to that platform. We were early – we've just had our six-year anniversary of Xero. But we probably only got it right midway through last year. So, we have four years of less than acceptable results, in terms of achieving our vision.

But, importantly, you were still a profitable firm during that time?

Yes, because the compliance aspect of our business is a luxury that not many industries have. Clients are still genuinely fearful of the tax authorities, so they do not want – in the case of New Zealand – to have the IRD jumping all over them. So, they are always going to look for expertise in that area. There is still good money that can be made from compliance and I think will continue to be made even with the technological improvements that we have seen.

So. is the winning formula giving clients quality advice, based on compliance? Because, unless taxation goes away, it seems that element will always be there. The tools will get better at helping put the pieces together, but you are still going to need that human element to say, "Well, here is what you should do." Is that your stance?

Definitely.

Tell us about how that human element helps out your clients in your advisory practice.

A lot of our clients are small business owners, like a husband and wife team – and they are so busy they spend all their time driving the bulldozer, instead of spending that one or two hours a week off the bulldozer actually looking at how best to drive their business forward. Helping them take that time is what our whole process does.

It's about having that investment in your people and that investment in the level five to six area to really drive that strategic stuff. A lot of time what you find is the "Now-Where-How" starts the process, but then the clients need more assistance to actually help them fully understand their 'big rocks', and appreciate that we are going to hold them accountable for achieving those big rocks. When they can see they are actually making tangible improvements to their business, they genuinely want to pay you to help them through that process.

To enable that, your team has got to have that of level of training, so we have invested a lot in to a level five to six advisory team that is now working flat out. We are now identifying people coming through the ranks that we think can operate in that area and spending a lot investing and training them and putting them in to networks where they can actually develop those skills very quickly.

How do you think this differs from other approaches to advisory, like consulting?

One of the things we talk about at WK is that we don't want to be seagulls. "Seagulls" are the old-style consultants that would come flying into a business, make a lot of noise, shit everywhere, then leave. They wouldn't make any substantial, lasting changes.

A mantra that we refer to all the time is "coaching not consulting". I don't like the word coaching, but it would be arrogant for us to think that we can go into a software company or a construction company or a trucking company or a retail business and know all the answers. We cannot.

What we can do, though, is have a really good understanding of business issues and ask lots and lots of questions, and help the clients reach the answers themselves by asking lots of really good questions. I use "Five Whys" all the time. It's simple - you ask Five Whys, one after another, and you get to the root of an issue. Or I use a rhetorical tool called the magic wand, which is: "No restrictions: if you had a magic wand, what would you change in your business?" That's a really good one, because it starts driving them to talk about their goals and their dreams.

It makes it sound quite easy!

In that respect, advisory is actually pretty easy! But that's where we naively thought, "Well, if advisory were that easy, then we should be able to implement across all of our team really quickly, and it shouldn't be a problem." So, we trained them all up on all of these things. How to do "Know-Where-Hows", "Magic Wands" and all of these other cool tools that we have access to via Mindshop. We went out and trained the team in all of this, but the mindset of a large percentage of the team wasn't quite right. So we unwound from that and, once we saw the pyramid, that was another a-ha moment for us. The moment was saying, "Let's actually use that pyramid, and get the right people working at the right levels." All of our team can do really good commentary, they can do really good clarity in presenting numbers better. A couple more can do that accountability piece. That then feeds our level six/seven team.

When it's all working together, it means the fee opportunity becomes really exciting for us, as a chartered accounting firm. For me, personally, what's even more exciting is the impact that I think it's going to have on our communities, and that it's going to make our regions a better place to live. That's really cool. That's why I do what I do.

Neil Stevens, WK

The big lessons: fail fast, make a big commitment as a team, and create a structure that puts advisory at the heart of the practice

Mistakes are inevitable, no matter how good the plan. Recognise that having your team on board and a good plan in place is about minimising the number and impact of mistakes, not eliminating them altogether. So, instead of avoiding errors, learn from the best while accepting that mistakes will happen – and when they happen, learn from that too. This is what separates the pacesetters from the pack.

"We made a strategic decision that we wanted to become advisors and we wanted advisory to be core and part of the DNA of WK. It hasn't necessarily always dropped to the bottom line – but has it made our clients more sticky? Has it improved the results we are helping our clients achieve? Has it improved our district as a place to live? The answer to all of those questions is yes, and that is what we are all about. That is what our strategy is all about."

FOCUS QUESTIONS AND ACTION ITEMS

Where are you now? Where are you trying to get to? How are you going to get there? Why are you trying to get there? What are you passionate about?

- Having goals is important, but understanding why you have those goals is vital. If you can work back from your goals to your "why", you'll have a much easier time of implementing change, and the change is more likely to stick. How do your existing goals relate to your "why" in practice? What goals might need to change to service that reason for being?

- **Take action:** Write down your personal "why", for your accounting job. If you don't yet know what that is, then write down your goals, and then work back from those to your "why". Don't be afraid to stop if things get existential, or even a bit weird. For instance, "I want to help green-tech startup companies to have the best possible chance of making positive change in the world" is just as valid, for a given individual, as "I want our practice to make us rich so we can all retire while young." It's your "why".

- Once you've got that down, think how it might apply across the rest of your practice. It can be a good exercise to take to the whole team, as a first step in drafting a genuinely meaningful mission statement or values that your practice will actually care about and work towards.

- Next, you can do one of Neil's favourite Mindshop exercises: a "Now, Where, How" for your firm. Where are you right now? Where do you want to go? How do you want to get there?

- Then identify **a**.) what key steps you need to take **b**.) who is going to do it and **c**.) when it's going to be done by.

Who in your practice is best placed to offer particular advisory services, to particular clients? And what tools will you use to deliver those services to clients?

- WK use an adapted version of Matthew "MC" Carter's value pyramid structure to break down advisory by a.) the personnel who can deliver particular levels of advisory services and b.) The tools they use in service delivery. Their whole app stack is built around this concept.

- **Take action – for larger firms:** If you're in a practice with more than five staff, do a staff segmentation exercise. If you are a partner or director, you can perform this exercise yourself, and/or do it as a team.

1. Make a list of all the advisory services that you can offer, or that you want to be able to offer.

2. Rank those services from most simple to most complex. Then map your practice staff to those tasks. Pay close attention to gaps in capability.

3. Once you've done this, map the tools you already use to the advisory services list. Again, pay attention to gaps. Note which staff members are proficient with particular tools.

Take action – for smaller firms or sole operators: If you have fewer than five staff, the above is still an exercise worth performing – but use it as more of a gap analysis. It may point the way to a firm specialisation or niche. If there are areas in which you or your staff are not proficient, these gaps can either be skills to train in, hire for, or avoid, so as not to spread yourself too thin.

12

INTRODUCING LIGHT-TOUCH ACCOUNTING ADVISORY SERVICES

By James Solomons, co-founder, Aptus Accounting

James Solomons runs a popular Australian advisory practice called Aptus Accounting, and is the former head of accounting at Xero. Here, he gives his advice on how to build out your advisory service offering.

Online accounting software is automating a lot of traditional accounting and bookkeeping tasks. Many accountants and bookkeepers are using the extra time to branch into advisory services. They're diving into business numbers and turning that data into insights. The line between accounting advice and business advice is blurring.

The firms and consultants who do this are becoming more ingrained in their clients' businesses. They provide more billable services and may even graduate to a year-round retainer.

An opportunity with challenges

The upsides are obvious, but it might not be practical for you to offer these services. Your clients might not show any interest in them, for a start. Or you may not have the resources to provide them. And adding services is not something you can do overnight. The transition process can be complex, requiring you to:

- scope new services and decide how to deliver them

- figure out how much to charge (and how much your clients will pay)

- communicate the benefits to your clients

- pilot the services at reduced cost to refine your offering

- update your marketing material

Plus you may have to get training or bring in extra resources to do the job properly. It's a big commitment.

ACCOUNTING ADVISORY SERVICES DON'T HAVE TO BE COMPLICATED

It's worth remembering that advisory services means a lot of different things to different people. Big-ticket advisory services like virtual CFO, business process improvement, and financial planning get the headlines, but you don't have to go to those extremes. Most businesses would benefit from far simpler advisory services.

A Xero study found that 65 percent of failed enterprises blame their closure on financial mismanagement. That includes things as simple as losing sight of cash flow.

For the many businesses struggling with these sorts of basic issues, you could make a world of difference by offering 'light-touch' advisory services. You could:

- help them choose some key performance indicators

- set up a dashboard to track those metrics

- use the dashboard to help them stay on track to achieve their business goals

WHAT ARE LIGHT-TOUCH ADVISORY SERVICES?

Light-touch advisory services are the first steps to a simple advisory offering.

You probably already give your clients advice – a phone call here, an email there. You may not always charge for it because it's ad hoc. But by setting up a simple dashboard, you can grow that offering into something more regular, and more billable.

- Share graphs of their cash flow situation and explain what it means for their business.

- Highlight revenue trends, or patterns of spending.

- Suggest ways in which resources can be deployed more efficiently.

- Show their progress against agreed KPIs.

This is a logical progression from the work you already do for your clients. It's really just identifying patterns and talking to your clients about them.

ADVANTAGES OF LIGHT-TOUCH ACCOUNTING ADVISORY SERVICES

A softer approach to advisory services works for you, and for clients. It can be introduced quite informally and you can build on it however you like.

Why it works for you

- Setting up the dashboard is simple with the right software.

- You can create a whole service around watching and reporting on the dashboard.

- You can tailor your services to client budgets – staying really light for smaller businesses.

- You'll get opportunities to troubleshoot business issues and sell extra services.

Why it works for clients

- You'll help cure the cash flow blindness that affects so many enterprises.

- They'll be able to make more informed decisions, right across the business.

- They'll have renewed confidence and peace of mind.

- You can ease them into it – so they don't have to spend more than they want.

Once you switch this service on – and clients begin to see the value in it – you can use it as a stepping stone to bigger things. Or you can simply limit your service to light-touch advisory services and outsource bigger issues to other firms or consultants.

SETTING UP A DASHBOARD IS STRAIGHTFORWARD – AND POWERFUL

Smart online accounting software comes with its own business performance dashboard which you can share easily with your client. If you set up bank feeds from the business account/s and use the same accounting software for invoicing, you'll get a powerful set of data, including:

- accounts receivable

- accounts payable

- cash reserves

- revenue over time

- expenses over time

- cashflow position

Millions of businesses have this simple data buried in paper records or on spreadsheets. Don't underestimate the value of making it accessible and visible. The true power of dashboards is that they make information actionable – giving you and your client at-a-glance analytics. That will give them a far greater sense of control, which is an incredibly valuable benefit to provide.

If you have a client with more complex needs, you can add an app such as Spotlight, Crunchboards, Fathom or Microsoft Power BI. These apps will integrate with the accounting software to track a wider variety of metrics and create more elaborate dashboards.

GROWING YOUR ACCOUNTS

Even if a client hasn't formally engaged you to track their KPIs, you can still look across this data quickly and comment where appropriate.

If you can see where things could be going better, it gives you an opportunity to make proactive, constructive suggestions. It's easy for you to do and shows you have a concern for their business. At the very least, it's a great courtesy to your clients. And it could be the first step towards a deeper consulting relationship.

DON'T FORGET THE ASSURANCE DASHBOARD

Business performance dashboards aren't the only online accounting tools that can grow your client relationships. The best accounting software packages also come with an assurance dashboard, which allows you to check on the activity happening in all client business bank accounts.

In a matter of minutes, you can review deposits, withdrawals and reconciliations to make sure everything checks out. It's a great way to identify unusual or suspicious activity in your client's Xero file or see if your client's getting stuck on something. For example, you can see how much time they're spending on bank reconciliations and offer to take it off their hands if it's too burdensome.

Turning accounting advice into revenue in four steps

It's easier to convince someone to pay for services once they understand the benefits. Here's how you can ease them into advisory.

1. **Get them set up**
   Invest a few minutes in each client and set their dashboard up for free. It's a relatively simple process for you, but the value for your client is enormous. They'll thank you for it.

2. **Decide on a pricing structure** Your client will be able to see the dashboard themselves, but propose a retainer for you to monitor it for them. The discipline of scheduled check-ins will ensure they make use of the extra insight.

3. **Delivering the service** Once you set up a dashboard and pull back the veil on your client's cash flow, they'll begin to see the real value of your service. Stay in communication. Call out interesting numbers and trends. Identify problems. If they haven't already decided on their KPIs, suggest a meeting to do that. It'll help keep them focused.

4. **Extra simple advisory services** If light-touch advisory services begin to lead into bigger projects, think carefully about how to handle that opportunity. You might outsource those jobs to a third party or do it yourself. If you do it yourself, you'll need a disciplined approach to figure out how to resource and deliver the new service.

A STEPPING STONE TO FURTHER ADVISORY SERVICES

Advisory services come in all shapes and sizes. There's no need to jump straight in at the deep end. You can start small, offering bite-sized advice that's valuable to your clients. And you won't have to radically restructure your firm to do it.

Remember that you already have an untapped resource – your own accounting experience. Light-touch advisory services let you generate new revenue based on that experience.

Soon your clients will wonder how they ever coped before they had access to your insight and wisdom. In this way, light-touch advisory services lead to better client relationships. And that means better business for you.

13

FIRST STEPS: ADVISORY SERVICES THAT WORK

by Richard Francis CA, CEO Spotlight Reporting
(Xero App Partner of the Year in 2015 and 2016)

Advisory by Choice & Advisory by Design

By now, you've hopefully made a conscious choice to supplement traditional work with additional, value-add services. This is one of the most important phases in the advisory journey; to actually make that philosophical commitment to offer more, do more and be more for clients.

To be advisory by choice is to engage the mind and heart in your work. The next step after being advisory by choice, is to be advisory by design.

Great advisory services don't exist in a vacuum; they are conceptualised, debated, nuanced and designed for release in market. Designing your services model around client needs, your own desires, and team skill-sets is a great approach to take.

GETTING CREATIVE

So what should you do? What can you do? A mash-up of these gives you: what *could* you do?

Service design can be messy – like most creative processes, there is a need to roll up the sleeves and mold the clay by hand. Squeeze and shape, add water and start again; it's a process of exploration and iteration.

Key questions to ask:

1. Can you do it? If not, what training and tools are required?

2. Can you learn it? If so, what's the best mechanism to do so?

3. Does the team – or possible strategic partners – have the expertise to supplement your own?

4. What do your clients (and prospects) think?

Whilst you shouldn't be *totally* driven by what clients want (or think they want), it certainly pays to ask the questions of your best customers.

DON'T BE SHY

If you're wanting to add value, share that fact far and wide. Offer "Business Growth" and "Profit Improvement" and "Advisory Board" and "Successful Start-Up" services face to face, on social, on your website and in your proposals. Don't be shy in sharing your advisory services, case studies and to get your advocates to spread the word.

The Big 6

As a CA and advisor for nearly twenty years, I found that the most successful core value-add services I offered when in practice were:

1. **Monthly mentoring** (with an emphasis on Spotlight-powered Virtual CFO analysis and insight) – this was recurring, ongoing contact/discussions that leads to flow-on work.

2. **Advisory boards** – get at the decision-making heart of client businesses, helping to shape the future and become Trusted Advisor.

3. **KPI setting** – measure what matters and report on this as part of the mentoring accountability loop.

4. **Decision-making support** – be on call, the go-to person for matters relating to goals and aspirations as well as nitty-gritty accounting

5. **Strategic planning and goal-setting** (with action plans) – help set the course, be a guide and broaden the discussion to unearth what really matters across business, financial and personal/family themes.

6. **Cashflow forecasting and budgeting** – put discipline around future planning, test the thinking, keep the bank and the Board happy.

These are all services that are useful in truly 'moving the needle' for your firm and for your clients. And, importantly, these are all services that most accountants can perform.

A rigorous focus on this menu of services helped us to move standard £2-3,000 per annum compliance jobs to £30,000+ per annum advanced reporting and mentoring relationships. Many of these relationships grew further and were long-term (startup to successful exit) by nature.

By journeying alongside our best clients as Trusted Advisors, we not only generated higher fee returns, but also deeper satisfaction on both sides. For our team, the advantages were:

- We were doing powerful work

- We felt that tangible value was being added

- Our skills were all being enhanced; and

- There was challenge and satisfaction for us all, every day.

So, let's now dive into some of these services in more detail:

MENTORING SERVICES

Accountants, with their professional education and continuing development, plus their ongoing exposure to business issues and opportunities, should be well-placed to adopt a mentoring role. Mentoring is essentially a relationship of guidance between someone with experience and expertise and someone who can benefit from those attributes.

Mentoring is rewarding, challenging work that adds real value and is the essence of what we can do if we choose to. It blends coaching, listening, nurturing and the development of 'soft skills' in the person or business being mentored, but is also a sharing of expertise around 'hard skills' like analysis, financial aptitude and sound business practice.

For my firm, mentoring clients to success was an essential daily element of our workflow. Customer success was more important than customer compliance.

Mentoring lends itself well to a regular cycle supplemented by 'as needed' interventions. Once a mentoring cycle is locked in, this rhythm provides a framework of mutual benefit.

My approach was to embed mentoring early and set the expectation of my involvement in the business. I established monthly mentoring as a service offering and used an agenda-driven approach to keep focus and ensure that we were asking the right questions that would lead us to discussion of opportunities and issues of importance.

One of the challenges of mentoring is to get the 'ground rules' laid early on. I always found that mentoring worked best when it went beyond being a cheerleader for the client, to a relationship where you could challenge and hold the client accountable. Sometimes this meant tough conversations and the parting of ways.

Ongoing mentoring should not only help support clients towards their aspirations, but deliver you an upside of regular fees and follow-on work. Mentoring is often integral to the DNA of value-add firms – and it could be for yours too.

ADVISORY BOARD

I have created and sat on numerous Advisory Boards, believing that aspirational businesses should not only be operationally sound but also be overseen by an experienced governance and accountability layer. This belief underpins why the establishment of Advisory Boards was one of our core value-add service offerings.

Ensuring that accountability and good governance are front and centre is just good business practice. It is a discipline and mindset that is best ingrained early, before too much can spin out of control or key requirements and responsibilities are overlooked.

Naturally one of the key disciplines of a Board - and one you can oversee from your seat - is reporting. The Virtual CFO has a lot to offer and should be an integral part of the Board membership.

Our Boards have always relied on the foundation of Spotlight Reporting and Xero. For good governance you need the accessibility of cloud accounting systems, but critically this and other data should be utilised as raw material for the analysis and insight of an integrated reporting system like Spotlight.

If, over time, you've been an integral part of the client journey as an advisor, when the time comes you just may get offered a seat on the formal Board of Directors as well. That of course raises the bar – and there are liability and other considerations to make – but it is certainly a good position to be in.

KPIs

Every credible business needs to measure what matters. Without the measurement of meaningful Key Performance Indicators, and a monitoring and reaction regime, your measure of success or otherwise becomes just a stab in the dark.

There are many opinions on critical KPIs for growth businesses, but we are seeing "smart growth KPIs" being borrowed from other industries such as software-as-a-service. The move to a more multi-faceted view than has traditionally been the case is opening up new areas of dialogue, as we found with Spotlight Reporting's WorkflowMax and Google Analytics integrations.

Thematically, we group KPIs like this:

- Engagement KPIs

- Revenue KPIs

- Team KPIs

An example or two for each follows:

Engagement KPIs
Net Promoter Score (NPS)

My view is that it is more dangerous not to engage with customer satisfaction trends and that our clients should proactively encourage feedback. To not do so is to miss out on useful analysis and suggestions for improvement, as well as revenue opportunities.

At Spotlight Reporting we use NPS on a rolling basis, allowing us to see satisfaction trends, and to receive immediate, actionable feedback. With NPS, follow-up is key – in fact, we see NPS primarily as a mechanism for improving dialogue and outcomes; every NPS respondent gets a call or an email and we absorb and utilise this feedback across our business.

Imagine if your firm did this and you inspired and coached your clients to do the same for their customer-base.

Community engagement

Community engagement is another facet for the modern business to monitor and react to. A battery of metrics can be tracked here:

- Electronic Newsletter open and click-through rates (find out industry averages and compare results).

- Website, blog and campaign landing page engagement.

Ultimately, you want to ensure that client discretionary activity and investment to engage prospects and existing customers actually converts into more satisfied customers, new revenue and greater loyalty.

Revenue KPIs
Average Revenue Per Customer (ARPC)

ARPC is a great indicator of:

- relationship depth and nuance

- client ability to offer, sell and deploy a range of services/products; and

- the ability to grow revenue faster than the absolute growth in customer numbers.

The great thing about ARPC is that once you understand the 'baseline' you can start planning for an increase. Each year you should be encouraging clients to think about the percentage increase in ARPC they aspire to, cross-referenced to the tactics and strategies they will deploy to achieve this. We used a similar approach at our accounting firm to get solid per annum ARPC growth over a number of years.

Team KPIs

Revenue per Employee

This is a solid KPI in wide use, and for me has more resonance than pure productivity measures that can be skewed by the individual. This measure gives a feel for:

- how smart the pricing, production and/or human interactions in the practice have been; and

- whether the top-line growth is moving at least as fast as the business head-count.

Report and React

Once you have selected your KPIs, regularly report and analyse them for clients, sharing your insight and embedding accountability. Program in client KPI monitoring and reaction regime – and make it a non-negotiable business process.

STRATEGIC PLANNING & GOALS

As a firm deepens its exposure to advisory jobs like virtual CFO work and mentoring, the opportunity to lead clients on their strategy formulation will almost inevitably follow. Your guidance and know-how should place you in a strong position to extend your remit into the strategic realm.

Strategic planning is a process undertaken at least annually by the smartest businesses. You want your clients to be as successful as possible, so suggest that they undertake strategic planning as part of their calendar of activity. Great planning requires a guide, facilitator, and/or professional expertise to be as robust as possible. If your clients are undertaking planning, you should be that guide.

True advisors don't just talk about the numbers, they set goals with clients and work alongside them to see the actions achieved. Setting goals is a powerful connector between accountant and client, preferably covering Financial, Business and Personal goals for a complete and holistic overview.

By talking goals, setting accountability for actions, and deliberately broadening the scope of conversation, you will get to the heart of what really matters. More meaningful conversations and setting goals in the correct context will help embed you as a trusted advisor and confidant.

PROCESS CREATES THE PLAN

Just as every good strategy and goal-setting exercise has some key elements, every good plan needs a process. In fact, I think the process is often just as important as the plan itself. I heartily recommend a strategic planning retreat with the key players; find a beach, lake or vineyard, incorporate some intellectual lubrication if preferred, and set an agenda.

The key elements in a good strategy normally incorporate:

- Vision

- Values

- Objectives/Goals - short term, medium term, long term

- KPIs

- Actions

- Owners

- Deadlines

It doesn't need to be much more complicated than that, but do invest the time and effort in doing this right – and make sure you charge for the tremendous value this process can create. A hungry business will need considerable fresh thinking, debate, research and late night conversations. Enjoy and embrace the process and you should end up with a good outcome for clients and your advisory practice.

CASHFLOW FORECASTING & BUDGETING

We all know that cash is the lifeblood of any business. Without liquidity, businesses wither and die.

Accountants and advisors are best-placed to do something about the massive liquidity problem in our small and medium-sized business sectors. With access to cash data and, crucially, the ability to project this forward so that businesses not only have an early-warning system in place, but can make smart decisions in a timely manner, **accountants should be putting cashflow forecasting at the heart of their advisory service offerings**.

My basic proposition to the accounting industry is that every business client deserves a cashflow forecast. Every business client deserves an understanding of cash and liquidity for better decision-making – and your care and attention as a trusted advisor to "make it happen".

Cashflow forecasting, therefore, should not be a marginal, on-demand proposition. Helping clients look ahead with confidence and to put in place basic cashflow maximisation strategies are core, essential and high-value activities for accountants to deliver on.

Cashflow Forecasting

This is perhaps the single most obvious and useful accounting output. It should also be the most profitable and valuable service, if done efficiently and sold with a 'value-based' mindset.

Forecasting doesn't have to be a big annual exercise, although a new trading year is a natural starting point. Periodic or 'rolling' forecasting – bringing in actuals and extending out the future view based on latest data and expectations – keeps the information fresh and relevant for good decision-making.

Remember, the customer is not just buying the forecast, they are buying your expertise and guidance. You are their cashflow 'navigator'.

Budgeting

The Budget often underpins the cashflow forecast, and can be seamlessly imported from Xero into Spotlight Reporting. A budget is a great touch-stone to determine (on an accrual basis), what the likely outcomes are for the year ahead (or beyond).

It is quick and easy to create a Budget using (and tweaking) last year numbers or from scratch. This is important for tax planning, remuneration planning for clients as well as for an understanding of what is possible.

Running scenarios allows you to consider 'conservative', 'status quo' or 'aggressive' numbers and strategies. This is all part of the risk vs reward thinking that businesses and their accountants too often side-step.

Cashflow forecasting and budgeting are cornerstones of business advisory

As an advisor, you and your clients will face many forks in the road. Opportunities or obstacles to consider, plan for and/or mitigate. With a Budget and Cashflow Forecast locked in, plugging in some scenarios – pricing changes, new revenue lines, margin improvements, OPEX control – is easy and illuminating.

A FINAL WORD ON FIRST STEPS

For the advisory services you offer to be credible, I recommend that you start close to home. Be your own advisor and analyst first. Adopt KPIs, report and react regularly, and be held accountable to your own Advisory Board.

Lock in a strategic plan every year, projecting accounting and cashflow numbers forward. Think about what is possible via exciting scenarios;

our own surveys indicate that substantial fee growth should be possible if you plan and deploy well.

The advisory opportunity is all about having applied and learned the skills on your own practice, and then the imagination to see it as an opportunity for clients. After that, you need the systems and software to support it; and the guts to do it – now!

Best of luck. And, of course, I suggest you start with Xero and Spotlight.

14

FINDING THE VALUE IN VALUES: LIVE CA BRING ADVISORY SERVICES TO LIFE

LiveCA's co-founders Chad Davis and Josh Zweig say the key to advisory is pretty simple: it all starts with the cloud. When everyone – client and staff - share the same data, it makes remote working not only possible but incredibly efficient. That's why all of LiveCA's clients are on Xero.

"Xero made this happen," Chad says. "From day one, Xero was the only accounting system we had ever used. Josh and I met, we started LiveCA, and Xero has been there through the whole ride."

"What's cool about using Xero is that when you have real-time data, you can have different conversations," Josh says.

For LiveCA, these conversations are the most vital part of how they structure their advisory offering, which is a core part of their hugely successful accounting practice. It's a big reason why they've been able to quickly grow from just the two co-founders to a renowned Canada-spanning practice with 80 staff.

MAKING ADVISORY REAL: "SELLING A MEETING"

A problem that many firms have with advisory services is that they are extremely difficult to define in terms of deliverables. What's the value to the customer? How can that value be communicated? What form do the deliverables take? And - perhaps most importantly – what's the cost to the firm of that deliverable? These are important questions for firms grappling with how best to offer advisory services, and LiveCA has found an innovative answer.

"As our business model continued to evolve, one of the things we started to effectively sell was a meeting," Josh says. "You can call it an advisory meeting, a management meeting, you can call it a part-time CFO – pick your lingo, but the idea is really to meet with a business owner more often, and talk through some of the things that are happening with the business. We go over the financial side, but also what's happening with the *story* of the business."

This concept of "selling a meeting", is a framework that Josh says is fundamental to LiveCA's approach to advisory services. Importantly, it ties in explicitly to the firm's fixed-price approach.

"When I say selling a meeting: well, we're doing fixed pricing. When you do a fixed price, you typically have to tie it to a deliverable. So, a deliverable *might* be monthly bookkeeping. It might be running your payroll. Those are some of the rudimentary tasks, and they're very easy to define," Josh says.

"But, when you look at the concept of business transformation, it's very hard to define on the cost side of things. It might take 40 hours for somebody to try to do this kind of advisory. It could take a more skilled person one hour to make the same kind of effect. So, it's really hard to define this in hours," Josh adds.

LiveCA's approach is to marry the two concepts, and make the deliverable the meeting itself, and then vary the meeting purpose depending on the client's needs at the time.

"You're going to meet once a month with your CPA, as a deliverable. The purpose of that meeting is, let's say, to go over the financials and maybe talk a little bit more in-depth about the business model. Over the next three to six months, if it turns out that you need more than that once-a-month meeting, we want to know why. Once we know why, we can then determine another deliverable," Josh says.

He cites a hypothetical example of a client who doesn't currently have an inventory system, so needs someone to help calculate margins on different SKUs and the cost of goods sold manually, and needs to talk to an advisor about this every week.

"So, that might be a deliverable, and all of a sudden you've defined a very ambiguous CFO meeting discussion to a specific goal for every single weekly meeting."

Josh says this system ensures their staff don't spend a large amount of time on ambiguous KPIs, and it helps prevent scope creep from impacting the firm's profitability.

"We're saying: here's the deliverable. It's a meeting. Here's what you expect to get out of that meeting. If, for whatever reason, we need much more time to get to that deliverable, we need to re-scope."

DO AUTOMATION AND CORE ACCOUNTING FIRST

On top of the Xero foundation, the LiveCA team has built a practice automation app stack that includes Receipt Bank for bookkeeping, and HubDoc for bills and core document management. Reporting tools like FUTRLI, Spotlight, Fathom and Float are sometimes used for scenario planning and specialist reporting. But when it comes to client apps, another of LiveCA's points of difference appears: they're highly methodical about how and when they introduce clients to apps.

"From a reporting perspective, we've worked with and have partnered with all of the reporting apps, but we've found it best not to throw an app at someone in the first three to six months."

The reason for this reticence is that LiveCA prefers to focus on client needs first, and this takes time. There are typically three or four things that are most important for any given company – cashflow concerns, systems, bookkeeping clean-ups, and how they price and collect their money. Because of this, the apps that LiveCA have their clients use at the start of the relationship all relate to core accounting functions and data automation. All the rest may be useful at a later stage – but that can wait.

"We never just throw apps at people. It's always with purpose. We're not going to set up budgeting tools. We're not going to engage in scenario planning. We're not going to do cash flow planning. We're going to understand why it's important for you, make sure we're measuring the right things, and then from there, figure it out," Chad says.

Fix core issues first, Chad says, and the rest can come later. Once those urgent issues are addressed, then further advisory app decisions can be made depending on whether the client needs information dissemination, calculation or interpretation.

BE SPECIALISTS, NOT GENERALISTS

LiveCA have learned that practices that want to focus on advisory can't be generalists when it comes to delivering something that businesses really, really want. Generalists, they say, tend to have high levels of competition, and find it harder to focus on delivering true value.

"We've enjoyed cultivating focused relationships," Chad says. "What that's meant over the years is we've had to change the structure of our delivery of services. So, before, where it would have been an accountant, a bookkeeper and a tech person, it's turned from a team of three to a team of six or seven."

Over the years, LiveCA has shifted their view of how services should be delivered to be highly specialist, as opposed to one accountant handling everything. Any given client will have a number of different specialists work on their account:

- A dedicated bookkeeper takes care of making sure the books are in great shape and that all transactions are coded and entered correctly

- An "in the weeds" CPA is tasked with looking after compliance work

- A treasury specialist is tasked with moving money, paying vendors, and making sure cash is received and spent in the most efficient way

- Payroll specialists are required to have knowledge of all local rules and regulations

- The tech team are app and technology specialists, who can help with onboarding, app selection, and designing new procedures and workflows when a new app is introduced

"We're not increasing the stress levels of traditional CPA's by encouraging them to become IT experts in this current environment. Instead, we're employing accountants that love tech. They live and breathe it, but they also might not have a background of a CPA – and that's okay," Chad says.

"Play to your people's strengths", Chad suggests. "If someone is great with people, then have them work with people. If someone's better at tax work and loves going deep into compliance, then encourage them to work on that. Once you've worked out what your current team members are good at, you're in a better place to analyse what skills your team is missing or that you want to hire for.

"People can love every aspect of accounting technology and not be an accountant, and we're lucky enough to have those people join our team, because here they get full reign to experiment and to put in new systems. That 'specialist' attitude has been what's made us, I think, a little bit different," Chad says.

DEFINING THE SCOPE FOR ADVISORY ENGAGEMENT

When a business asks for advice, they often don't know exactly what it is they need help with, besides recognising the need for help itself.

Often, a customer will effectively be saying "I don't know what I'm doing, so I'm going to pay someone to tell me what to do." While this is an enormous opportunity for advisors, it leaves open the question of what work the advisor is actually going to do. LiveCA say it's very important to pin down the scope of what a given advisory service or meeting will provide.

"If you won't define what it means to be a part-time CFO or what it means to have a monthly discussion with a customer, you could have this mismatch of expectations," Josh says. "A customer might say, 'Well, I thought you were going to give me advice on fundraising or pricing," or all these different facets of business. Well, you might need 30 years of experience [in their business] in order to be able to do that!"

When it comes to defining scope for advisory engagement, the most important thing is that the advisor recognises the area in which they can be of most help to the business, and then tailors the advice accordingly.

"Today, we're far better at determining what the scope of an engagement looks like and what we think is valuable for the customer. If we're going to offer some type of advisory, we make it very clear what this looks like," Josh says.

"A lot of times when the customer is ambiguous like, 'Oh, I don't know where I need help.' We're not going to sell that customer help when we can't define it. So, it might go something like – you know what, first let's work together in the financial op side. Let's see how the business is doing, and then we'll be able to ask you some questions to scope what an advisory relationship could look like. We sort of make it a step-by-step process, versus an all-encompassing, we'll transform your business.

DON'T LIMIT YOUR IMAGINATION OR IMPOSE FALSE BOUNDARIES ON WHAT'S POSSIBLE

Xero has many remarkable accounting and bookkeeping partners all over the world, but LiveCA stands out as a bright beacon of what imagining what's possible and then really doing it.

LiveCA's approach is truly exciting and radical: they are a fully-distributed firm, where all the staff work remotely, and there's no central office. This remarkable paradigm extends across the business, and includes the way they do advisory services; with an unerring focus on client needs. While you may never wish to replicate their 100 percent virtual business model, there is so much to learn about how approaching the same client-accountant relationship from a different vantage point can teach all of us.

WHAT ADVISORY MEANS TO LiveCA

Josh says the first time that he realised the sheer impact that advisory services could have on clients lives was when he attended a client's birthday party on a cruise ship, where he bumped into one of the client's close friends.

"I met her and she said, 'My god, you're Josh. You know, the only two people who Chris ever quotes are his mother, and you.' I think that was the first time I recognised how much of an impact I had. I guess I never really considered it, because it was part-and-parcel of what I did. I realised that this stuff does have a significant impact, and in a way, I was acting as a mentor to this person."

Once they had figured out that advisory services were something they could sell and deliver on, LiveCA sold a price plan to a new client who was taking over a consulting business that was virtually bankrupt. They met with the client monthly, and within 18 months, the business had gone from going bankrupt to a $10 million dollar turnover. Josh took the opportunity to ask the client how he felt about this astonishing turnaround.

"In a very modest way, he was able to attribute some of this success to the discussions we had," Josh says. "It's very rewarding to sort of feel part of that success. Normally, the accountant is quite distanced from the finances.

Here, it was something that you could actually share in some success and feel pride that you were able to really help somebody do this."

The way LiveCA looks at advisory is that it can be separated into two buckets. They call the first bucket "tech" – meaning putting a client's financial workflow on the cloud.

"That's effectively the core of what we sell. You can demo that, because it's tangible. You can look at a case study and say, hey, we took a customer from desktop Sage, to being able to see their data in real time," Josh says.

The second bucket is what LiveCA like to think of as mentorship, or coaching. This, they say, is harder to describe, because it's both more intangible and harder to do – but there is a way to do it right. This requires a customer who understands the value of the advice on offer, and an advisor whose expertise is in sync with the customer's needs.

"I think advisory is a bit flawed in the sense of [people think] it means that 'oh, I'm supposed to give this advice.' I think true advisory is very similar to coaching, where you're meant to ask the right questions to guide someone to their own conclusions. To get there you need a certain type of customer, whose success the advisor can unlock. In order to do this properly, advisors need to realise it's valuable, and customers have to recognise that it's something they need," Josh says.

KEEP RELATIONSHIPS TIGHT

In keeping with their holistic approach to advisory, LiveCA prefers to keep their specialist services in-house. While it's not the only way to do things – many firms successfully outsource large chunks of their tasks – Chad suggests that for LiveCA, it's easier, and more valuable to the customer, when everything's under one roof. Except that in LiveCA's case, it's a virtual roof.

"In a traditional CPA firm relationship, there are multiple people involved. A tax CPA, an outside bookkeeper and maybe an employee at the company. In our experience, this has led to a lot of finger pointing and we wanted to fix that by design," Chad says. "We think that when every financial aspect is under one firm's purview, it increases accountability, clarity and the feedback loops that make the relationship stronger over time."

If your firm isn't in a place where everything can be done in-house, it's still possible to keep relationships with contractors and outsourcers tight. Act like a virtual firm, make the most of the cloud and connectivity, and make sure that you choose your relationships carefully. If you are outsourcing, the people you're outsourcing to should feel like part of your team.

COMPLIANCE IS A FOUNDATION ON WHICH INCREDIBLE ADVISORY CAN BE BUILT

A crucial factor in LiveCA's success in offering advisory services is the recognition that compliance and advisory are part of the same continuum. The need for clients to stay legal and tax-compliant feeds the data that feeds the advisory. In a holistic approach, forward-looking advisory services and past-looking compliance bleed into each other. This is so much the case that LiveCA hesitate to quantify how much of their service is advisory and how much is compliance. To them, it's all part of the advisory package.

"The way we sell services is all-encompassing. We're saying for this price, you'll get all of these things, so we don't necessarily list out individual items," Chad says.

"So, you could say that the advisory/compliance split at LiveCA has a very large focus on what you typically call compliance, because we typically see people that are coming from a place of having information that isn't correct, no information at all, or just information they don't trust."

"But it's more than just compliance – if we were just going to be a firm that was delivering compliance, we wouldn't pay over a million dollars in tech team salaries," Chad adds, laughing.

A better way of framing the advisory/compliance divide is that helping clients to trust and understand their data is vital to the success of any advisor-client relationship.

"When it comes to having trust in the data, well, what does that really mean? For us, it means documentation, truly understanding workflow constraints, and reviews by technical and tax professionals. But to customers, it could mean different things to different people," Chad says. "That's why it's important for us to be close with every customer and understand what's important to them. For some it could mean matching cost of goods sold with relevant revenue numbers and for others, it could be how accurate every expense is allocated to the GL."

LiveCA say they've never gone out to market to sell advisory services in a traditional sense. Instead, they've concentrated on being a vital part of each business that they advise – actually taking part in creating the data, and immersing themselves in understanding what the numbers actually mean for the business. Advice then naturally follows as a part of this relationship.

"We've always wanted to be part of the team that creates and manipulates the data, so we can actually have conversations that mean something, versus conversations that pick out sore points and finger-point at someone else to make yourself look smarter," Chad says.

"At the end of the day, if you're focusing on what's important to them and really caring about the product you're delivering, it doesn't get much better than that."

BE CHOOSY WHEN SELECTING CLIENTS - AND STAFF

Another factor that makes LiveCA a very different kind of practice is that they are incredibly choosy when it comes to selecting clients.

"We probably send away seven out of every 10 people that contact us, Chad says. "Of those three, we might take a second call with one, and from there we bring them on board as a client."

Chad cites Baker's Law on customer selection: bad customers drive out good customers. Many accountancies still have a strictly local focus, and while that's not necessarily a bad thing in itself, it can lead to firms taking on nearly every client that comes along. This most certainly is a bad thing. Your worst customers will take up a disproportionate amount of your practice time and mental energy. How to avoid this? Either agree to a parting of the ways – or better yet, don't engage with them in the first place.

LiveCA makes sure they bring on good clients by scoring them on key criteria as they relate to the client's values.

"We look at every interaction based on four criteria: The communication skills of the person that we're working with, their attitude towards life and towards accounting in general, their ableness to work and how much they're willing to put into the work," Chad says. "So, if you take those four attributes and assign values for every incoming person, you can almost foreshadow how successful the relationship will be. It's not always perfect, but those are the four things we look for before signing on anyone."

This careful approach to people also applies, more stringently, to how LiveCA select staff to work with. Staff are selected on values and aptitude, not necessarily how long they've been working or how much industry experience they have. Accounting skills, if they're lacking in any way, can always be learned on the job. LiveCA also has a vigourous 2-day trial work day process that brings people 'in' and puts them through an online course they developed. This allows the candidate to be objectively tested, to see what it's like to work remotely and most importantly, to meet some of the team.

"Today, we're at 60 team members. Over the time we've been in business, we've received about 15,000 applications to work with us, and we have only selected a little over 80 to work over the last five years," Chad says.

MAKE VALUE THE FOCUS, AND GROWTH WILL FOLLOW

LiveCA take the same approach to their staff as they do to clients: it's all about first finding a values match, and from there *adding* value to their lives. Rather than focusing on growth, and using that as the single most important metric for success, LiveCA sees their firm as being on a journey. There's no one destination, but there's plenty to be learned along the way.

"Whenever I talk to other firm owners about growth, a lot will say, 'Oh, it's cool how much you've grown.' For us, we don't really see it as a growth," Chad says. "We don't focus on the numbers. We focus on the tiny minutiae, the details that it took to get there."

"If LiveCA were a traditional company with investors," Chad says, "we'd be told to chase the money and grow, grow, grow." While this approach has plenty of merits, especially for venture capital-funded startups, LiveCA has found it more rewarding to focus first on the team, enabling flexible hours, remote work, family time, and professional development. And it's another reason for their careful approach to selecting clients; it helps their staff live their best work lives.

"If the team is working with customers that are mean, or don't value what they're doing, why even bother? You could get that at any other firm. You could do it by yourself by going out and grabbing any client that needed accounting services," Chad says.

"There has to be a reason why people join us to work, but also join us as a customer. So, we have to stand for something. I think what we stand for is a very respectful, challenging workplace for people that want to support each other and grow together. For customers, we stand for quality work, delivered remotely, in a day and age where on average, it's really tough to have accurate information."

"This approach has helped bring on the right team members and the right customers and when you get that right, work is so much more enjoyable," Chad says.

HOW LIVECA DOES PRICING

Every customer is priced individually

All LiveCA's engagements are on an agreed-upon fixed price, monthly recurring basis with no long term commitment. The work that they do is specific to a customer's particular business model and financial workflow. LiveCA have a three-call discovery process in determining a scope of a project so they can then provide three potential pricing options to choose from:

1. Clients get on a call with a LiveCA CPA to go through a high-level discussion of their accounting processes, including invoicing and expense tracking, to ensure they address all the tax compliance needs.

2. Next, clients have a chat with the Live CPA tech team to go over the system side of the business and dig into the roles and responsibilities of the engagement. At this stage, LiveCA may suggest a number of apps that may help the client automate or streamline some of the mundane accounting functions. If the client's already set up with good systems, LiveCA will take the time to gain a solid understanding of the system to make sure they can help.

3. Clients will get a choice of three plans that have been designed specifically for them. These plans typically include all their year-end tax and compliance documents, unlimited support, and the price of technology and apps, plus extras depending on the clients wants or needs.

"We've never had fixed costs or fixed prices. Nothing is based off a menu. Every single relationship is priced differently with a different deliverable, with different timelines and different tech stacks. So, it's not incredibly scalable, but at the same time, it's really valuable to the right customer," Chad says.

The LiveCA client workflow: from onboarding to ongoing

- Initial sales video call

- Tech demo video call

- Pricing video call

- Onboarding video call (login to apps, gather docs, etc.)

- Manager video call (tax planning, set priorities and deliverables now that work is starting)

- Work starts and is ongoing from there

LiveCA Team Structure / CLIENT SERVICE TEAM

This is a typical team that an average LiveCA customer would work with.

Client Service Team structure: LiveCA's flexible structure and approach means the composition of a client service team can vary depending on the client's need, but this is an example of a typical structure and workflow that works well for the average client

BECOME INDISPENSABLE BY WORKING YOURSELF OUT OF A JOB

One fear that many accountants have about advisory services is that it will lose them clients over the long run. Surely, the reasoning goes, accountants are in the business of profiting from complexity. What if you reduce business complexity too much, or make the job look too easy? Can you do too well at advising clients? Won't it mean that you advise yourself out of a job?

"That's looking at it the wrong way," says Josh.

"If you look at any profession, I argue that the job of the professional is to work themselves out of a job. If you think otherwise – if you're a doctor, and you're like 'I want this guy to see me more, so I'll tell him to eat margarine every day,' I'd say you're a bad professional."

Advisors should back themselves to be relevant and useful to the client. For the most part, clients will value the relationship *much more* than they otherwise would. But if the client ends up not needing the accountant, that just means the advisor's done their job well – and more business will follow from that.

"The idea is to make your patient, or the client, healthy and self-sufficient. That should be your goal. If you've got a good business model, then you'll be able to charge the right amount so you can still profit from it and have a sustainable business. The goal should be a happy customer who will refer their friends to you."

Chad agrees. To everyone at LiveCA, the most important thing about their jobs is adding value to people's lives, and it just so happens that advisory services are the best way to accomplish that.

"I don't think it matters what you call yourself. It really just matters how customers feel after they've gotten off a video chat with you," Chad says.

"So, do we consider ourselves an advisory firm? Sure, because we're taking someone from a place where they had an issue, walking them through some possible solutions, deciding on it with them and then implementing it. I don't think you can get more advisory or consultative than that."

Meet the Advisors: Q&A with Chad Davis and Josh Zweig

When Xero caught up with LiveCA co founders Chad Davis and Josh Zweig, Chad called from an RV park on the west coast of Canada, and Josh from an Airbnb in Argentina. But neither of them were on holiday. Chad works out of an ample-sized RV he shares with his wife and two small children, and Josh from whatever city he happens to be in – the week before, he was in Toronto, and before that, Buenos Aires. It felt like a radical insight into a remarkable new way of working.

"Josh and I had two reasons for starting this company," Chad says. "One, we wanted to bring something to the market that hadn't been done before, regardless if it crashed and burned or not. No one was really doing accounting services on a larger scale in a remote company."

As he talks, noises drift in from outside – the sound of his children playing in the campground, set against the ocean breeze.

"Two, we wanted to get out of work something that was deeply personal. For me, that meant spending time with my family, having another child, those traditional things you do. We wanted to be able to have a firm that stood for this new way of working, which was that you can work location-independent and still have some strong relationships. If people are willing to work with you, based on the merits of the work you do and what you stand for, then if it works great, and if it doesn't, hey, at least you gave it a try."

First things first – Chad, tell us how you came to be living in an RV!

Chad: After five years of gruelling work and putting in a lot of long hours, I got to a point where I was missing important time with my family – but I was still just as interested in work! So, last year I bought a 32 foot (9.7m) RV, went across Canada, came back home and said, "That was amazing." I got to meet employees, see customers, but it was only for the summer.

So I thought: how can I do this full time?

So, I bought a bigger RV (42 ft or 12.8M) with a fully enclosed office and I've been on the road for half the year, and there's no plans (today) to go back to the house. It's rented out. We're homeschooling our kids on the road. We're putting them in programs in every city we stop in, for things like skating, dance and art classes. I'm meeting team members I've never met in person before and it's incredible. Canada is a beautiful place and getting to live in different cities really shows how diverse and amazing this country really is. The experiences that I've gone through in the last three or four months (surfing, whale watching, mountain biking, boating, etc.) have been so different to the last five years and I hope it's creating family memories that we'll never forget.

Business time: Tell us about some of the mistakes you've made on your advisory journey to where you are today

Josh: I think one of the mistakes that we made was overselling our services, or rather, not defining what the deliverable is that you're going to get for that kind of service.

There there is a tremendous value in streamlining financial operations, a tremendous value in regular discussions with customers and up-to-date bookkeeping and just understanding the financial outlook of the organisation, and a lot of businesses don't have that. I don't want to down play that. But if you won't define what it means to be a part-time CFO or what it means to have a monthly discussion with a customer, you could have this mismatch of expectations. When a customer says, "Well, I thought they were going to give me advice on fundraising or pricing," or all these different facets or business – well, you might need 30 years of experience in order to be able to do that.

So, I think that was a mistake we made for a time period without defining that. Today, we're far better at determining what the scope of an engagement looks like, and what do we think is valuable for the customer. If we're going to offer some type of advisory, we make it very clear what this looks like.

Tell me about the tech stack that you use, and how you implemented it

Chad: Sure. So, the tech stack today is different to the tech stack was three years ago and that was different than the tech stack five years ago. But it gets really hard to change when you get larger. So, when we had five to 10 people and we were switching from – I even forget the name of the tool we had before Slack – it was a quick move. You flicked it on and you showed the five people the new way of working and you were done in an afternoon. Well, now the firm is 50 or 60 people, so it takes months of planning to bring in a major new practice management component.

What are some of the advantages of remote working?

Chad: First and foremost, for the staff, when spouses or family members move, they can now move. They don't have to lose a job that they love. I love that part. The second thing is families. For new families, with a young child or someone coming off of maternity leave, a mother or a father, it's about being able to provide a working environment where they can come back to work, still be with their children, and not give up on those really early years that are so incredibly important for the development of the child. We're actually playing a positive role in the way that kids can be brought up now. As a father of two, I think that one of the coolest things about working here is that families can now stay together longer, when one of them is working at LiveCA.

The other things we do is, for people that don't have families, they can travel, and we pay for it through stipends. We give staff a travel allowance every year and they can get together. Right now, there are trips being booked in Costa Rica, Aruba, and places like that for next month. Our CTO travelled to 22 different countries and worked in almost all of them doing a work-cation for almost a year. We've got military families here, where some are being stationed around different parts of Canada, and they're able to just pack up and move and it doesn't matter where they get sent. So, it's less stress on them.

It sounds incredible, but there must be drawbacks, right?

Chad: The trade off is that you have a slower net income growth rate. You're spending and spending and spending, and you're preparing for the growth. I think if we weren't okay with it and we chased profit in the early years to a point where it consumed us, we would have never grown or probably felt the same way we do about our team and the way we're growing. But, because we've had that team-first approach, we have to live it. By living it, you make less money at the end of the day, because you're spending it on things that are important to you. So, that's the drawback. The drawback is you aren't able to invest even more back into the things that are important to you.

But on the flip side, if you had a lot of employee turnover because you were chasing revenue, the cost of that turnover is just exponential to the salary of somebody that you're actually replacing. So for us, we're hoping and betting on this business model, because not too many people are doing it quite this way, to this extent. I'd love to be a case study for professional services that shows it's possible to run a firm that's respectful and grows respectfully, but at the same time can be profitable and does so with a good conscience towards all our team members that choose to work with us.

So how has this way of doing things all come about? Is it a planned thing, or is it more organic?

Chad: Creating this different type of business model is not one or two people. It's the evolution of everybody's ideas that have come from the entire team. What's amazing is that if someone in the firm has a great idea, it's "best idea wins". We're not trying to be top-down in this sort of really strict way of running things. Even though a lot of decisions have to be made, I think what makes it work is that people can feel like their voice is heard, and they keep doing it because changes are made after people come up with great ideas.

Seeing as this way of working has been doing well for you and your firm, how are you spreading the idea around?

Chad: It's great being part of government and professional body meetings and committees and round tables. It's like having a voice for the generation that cares more about their team than partner profits. It's a really fun thing for both Josh and I to be a part of. We're both on CPA Canada and CPA Ontario committees, and being able to share how we work, how we're structured and how we think with a group of people that are shaping our profession is really important to us. Where it might be table stakes for you and I today, it's not for the industry.

If somebody sees this five or ten years down the road and says, "Oh, I'd like to build a firm like this." I think that's healthy for the industry. Customers are going to have a really great accounting experience and in turn, they may slowly change the way they think about accountants. If we can play any role – no matter how small – in changing people's perceptions of what accountants are and how we can help, I think that's the bigger end game here.

Chad Davis, Live CA

The big lessons: advisory does have concrete deliverables – they're meetings; make sure you define the scope for advisory engagement; and choose your clients by value matches

FOCUS QUESTIONS AND ACTION ITEMS

How can I sell a meeting to clients?

If your accounting practice is like most, then you'll have clients with questions they want answered. Of those, many will want advice on how to grow and maintain their businesses.

Take action: If you've worked through other action items and you know which clients want your help, you can reach out to them to work out the way to best deliver that assistance. The clients who can benefit most will want regular contact and accountability, and you can set up a series of meetings at a frequency that will work for the client's business to deliver that. Remember, the meeting itself is the deliverable – it is up to the client to make the most of your advice.

Take a step back from the day-to-day, and ask yourself this important question: What advice would you give to your own practice, if they were a client asking for help?

• If you were your own clients, there's a very good chance you'd advise yourself to get your data in good order. For an accounting practice, the best way to do this is with apps that automate data capture and flow. Our data shows that adopting apps that focus on delivering practice efficiencies first is by far the best way to achieve rapid growth. This includes apps that do:

- Automated data extraction

- Online job/practice management

- Automated payables management

- Online compliance workflow

- Automated client communications

- Financial analysis and forecasting

Take action: What are your biggest pain points? What are the things you struggle most with in your practice, or that your staff find difficult? Have a private brainstorm, or if you're feeling brave, maybe gather everyone around for a gripe session where you all get to dish on everything wrong in the practice!

Make a list of all the pain points, rank them order of worst to least pain, and then identify which have to do with information capture, flow and analysis. Chances are, there's a cloud app that works well with Xero that's built to tackle that specific problem – and having a hierarchy of difficulties also helps your practice decide in what order you should adopt them.

Do I, or my practice, share the same values and goals as my clients?

If you have established what your practice's "why", or reason for existing is, and you know what your mission and values are, and those are shared by your staff, you can look to see if those values are shared by your clients.

Take action: As with most other things in advisory, the way to ascertain this is through contacting your clients. When you are meeting with them, it's a chance to ask about their values and their mission. If they can clearly encapsulate this, it's a good sign. Chances are, you'll be able to find common ground.

Make sure you and your staff have the ability to take note of clients who are difficult, or who are having difficulty. While accounting practices for years have taken nearly every client who comes along, this no longer needs to be the case. Sometimes, some people simply aren't meant to work together. If you know what your values and mission are, you can use this as a basis to identify clients who don't match and take the opportunity to go your separate ways.

For new clients, the initial engagement is the opportunity to find out if they're a good match for your firm. Make sure whoever meets with new clients is empowered to make a value judgement. If the client's values and goals are a match, it's likely they will be a good client. If they're not, they can politely be moved on, or referred to another firm.

15

10 WAYS TO EVALUATE ACCOUNTING FIRM PERFORMANCE

You use data and benchmarks to measure the health of your clients' businesses. But are you evaluating your own firm's performance? Use the following metrics to see how your business measures up.

METRICS THAT CUT TO THE HEART OF CLIENT SERVICES

Service industries are all about clients. Are you making them happy? Are they making you profitable? You need metrics that cut to the heart of those questions. Here are some simple measures you can take to rate firm performance.

1. Are clients staying?

It's important to maintain a healthy client base with consistent revenue. Watch these indicators to see how you're doing:

- the rate of increase or reduction in your total client base

- how long clients stay with your firm

- how often you acquire new clients

- why they leave

- the strength of your client relationships

The expense of acquiring new clients dwarfs the cost of keeping old ones. Some sources say it costs between five and ten times as much. So while some turnover is unavoidable, you'll want to keep it in check.

Do you know who your most profitable clients are? Make sure you look after them. You can improve retention by cross-selling other services to them and regularly reviewing your offerings to make sure you stay relevant to their business.

2. How happy are your clients?

About 60 percent of small businesses who answered a survey by The Sleeter Group said they were highly satisfied with their accounting firm, but 20 percent were dissatisfied. Could 20 percent of your clients be unhappy?

You can reduce the likelihood of dissatisfaction by developing a system to invite and track client feedback. Ask if they're happy with the quality of work, the level of service and the loyalty you show them. Start with your key clients.

You can ask them face to face – some clients will like that approach – but use online surveys where you can. It makes it easier for respondents to be honest. And it's honesty you need. Open yourself up to the process. Encourage clients to be candid. If there are problems out there, you're better off knowing about them.

3. Do your new clients love the experience you provided in their first two months with your practice?

The onboarding experience is of huge importance to clients. First impressions count, and they're likely to be lasting. If you make the client onboarding experience smooth and as enjoyable as possible for your client, they'll be singing your praises. If not, even great service down the line may have trouble making up the difference.

The importance of onboarding is more than just common sense, too.

In a Xero UK survey of 1500 randomly selected small businesses, of those who said they were planning to change accountants, a staggering 75 percent said that a negative onboarding experience was a factor in their decision to switch.

The good news is that when it comes to making your onboarding experience great, the cloud matters. A lukewarm 58 percent of businesses surveyed reported a positive experience being onboarded to a desktop-based accounting system with a new accountant, versus *100 percent positive experiences* of those brought on to cloud accounting, with a new accountant.

The message is clear: for a great new client experience, never move them to anything but online accounting.

4. Are you making the most of your existing clients?

Could you be under-serving some of your clients? Think about their potential value compared to their current value. If there's a gap, work out how to close it. Calculate the costs of moving clients to more profitable services. There might be some short-term pain but the investment could be worth it.

To find out where the profitability is in your firm, calculate the annualised revenue per client, per service. Some revenue streams will look good. Others might not. Once you know which types of clients and services make money, you're better placed to set a strategic direction for the firm.

5. Do you monitor your clients' needs?

It's a good habit to check in with your clients regularly. It's a common courtesy and a good way to reinforce the value of your services. Always make contact using your client's preferred method. Some like in-person meetings, others would rather have phone calls, texts or use online chat.

Be sure to track all these communications so you can build on past conversations without repeating yourself. Regular, thoughtful contact improves client satisfaction and retention, and it makes it easier to upsell additional services. Set goals to have these sorts of big-picture talks periodically.

6. Do you update your services?

Make sure you're offering the right services to your clients. Ask what they need. It shows you care about their business. It's even better if you suggest what they might need, because that shows you not only care, but you also understand their business. Pick a client every week and call them to see if they need support with bookkeeping, payroll, or business consulting.

Besides offering new services, tell clients how you can improve existing interactions. New technologies constantly change how business is done. Tell them how those developments can improve accounting. You could offer virtual CFO services, for example. Your clients will be reassured that you're on top of those sorts of trends.

Whenever you change your offering, make sure to communicate it well. Use blogs, newsletters, seminars and social media to bring your clients on the journey. But don't forget to communicate personally, too. Not everyone has the time to follow your blog.

7. How responsive are you?

How long does it take your staff to follow up client requests? Each client will have different expectations. You should know what those expectations are and whether or not you're meeting them.

Clients like things to be actioned quickly. It shows you take them seriously. Motivate your staff to be responsive and make sure your internal processes don't slow them down. Replace outdated systems and remove workflow bottlenecks. It could take your firm's performance to the next level.

8. Do your clients work at your pace?

Responsiveness is a two-way street. Measure the time it takes clients to respond to your staff's requests.

Your firm can only be as productive as your clients allow you to be. You might have to work two or three times harder to complete a piece of work with a difficult client – and that can really hurt profitability. If you have clients who slow you down and distract you from profitable work, it might be better to let them go.

9. Are your staff productive – or just busy?

Are you making the most effective use of your most valuable resource – your staff? You probably don't bill by the hour anymore, but it's still worth measuring staff utilisation to health-check your business. It'll show how your people are using time and will reveal if effort is being wasted on unproductive tasks. Who knows – a simple change in process could save hours of time and boost firm performance.

Remember, though, that utilisation rates will vary between staff members. Partners can spend as little as 50 percent of time on billable work due to managerial and business development responsibilities.

10. Where's the profit coming from?

All firms measure revenue and profit, and most have a projected growth target. Those numbers are only a crude measure of firm performance, however. To get a truer sense for your future, measure the projected and actual revenue growth of different parts of your business, such as:

- individuals or teams within your firm

- business groups or units in your firm

- the segments or industry sectors you serve

- your firm's key service offerings

Being categorical in this way will help you identify where the potential lies in your firm, and which areas need rethinking. You may even consider reducing or dropping some services if they're unprofitable or consistently trending downwards.

KEEP EVALUATING FIRM PERFORMANCE TO FIND GROWTH OPPORTUNITIES

When you run an accounting business – and you see the books weekly – it's easy to think you have a good handle on firm performance. But put intuition aside and try a formal review. Pull some of the numbers suggested here and take a deeper look. It's good discipline and you might just be surprised at what you find.

If certain services or clients are working for you, nurture them. When they're not, consider strategic change. It's not complicated. It's just a matter of making the time to do it. Reviewing firm performance using these simple metrics could be your first steps to renewed profitability.

16

HOW TO SELL ADVISORY SERVICES TO YOUR CLIENTS

Many firms struggle to actually sell advisory services to their clients. This is because the quality of selling skills needed to sell advisory skills is much higher than the quality of selling skills needed to sell compliance services. This is why this chapter, written by Heather Townsend, Author and Founder of **The Accountants Millionaires' Club**, looks at the practical selling skills you will need to learn to convert the opportunities that come your way.

"Half the battle is selling music, not singing it. It's the image, not what you sing." **Rod Stewart**

Why is selling advisory services much harder than compliance services?

It's pretty simple: when it comes to compliance services, your clients have no choice but to buy them. They may huff and puff about it, but – often by law – they are compelled to buy these services. As a result selling compliance services tends to be fairly simple. You know clients need these services, and clients know you can provide them.

When it comes to selling advisory services, it's different. Advisory services are optional. Sure, you know their business would run better if they created and followed a business plan, but there is usually no legal or regulatory reason why they need to have a business plan. And even if your client knows they need a business plan, there is no reason why they can't either a.) do it themselves or b.) pay a different professional, perhaps a business coach, to help them with their business plan. By way of example, the following steps on their own will be ineffective to get your clients to buy advisory services from your firm:

- Putting your advisory services on your website

- Adding your advisory services to a proposal

- Telling your clients that you offer these services on an email

Unfortunately, when it comes to selling advisory services, that's all a lot of firms do.

To sustainably sell advisory services you need to:

- **Identify there is a need** for your firm's advisory services in the first place

- **Qualify this need** to see whether they are **a**) serious about doing something about it, and **b**) if their requirements and budget match what your firm has to offer

- **Demonstrate the value** of your firm's advisory services

- **Increase the motivation** of your client to buy

How to identify there is a need for your firm's advisory services

When it comes to selling advisory services, you are looking for commitments from your client or prospect that they are interested. This could be as simple as them telling you they think they need your firm's services. Or it could be that they agree to have a chat when you suggest a given advisory service, in response to them telling you about a problem they have. However, life is rarely that simple. Very often you will have good potential clients for your advisory services right under your nose. You just need to look and listen a little harder. For example, good candidates for advisory services might include:

- Clients who are very similar to another client of yours who has already bought advisory services from your firm

- Clients who regularly visit your website, particularly the 'about us' and 'pricing page'

- Clients who open and read most of the emails you send to them

- Clients who enjoy using you as a sounding board or want to pick your brain regularly

At the simplest level, the best way to find out if your existing clients need your firm's advisory services is to maintain a regular dialogue with them. In this dialogue you want to discuss their progress and challenges they are facing to achieve their personal and business goals.

HOW TO QUALIFY A POTENTIAL CLIENT FOR YOUR ADVISORY SERVICES

Before you book a time-consuming meeting with a potential client for your advisory services, you want to qualify them. Without qualifying them you risk wasting oodles of time on people that are either never going to take your advisory services or will prove to be the wrong type of client.

—

PAUL MILLER'S ADVISORY STORY

We are very picky about the type of client we take on. This means we spend a lot of time qualifying our leads. When we receive a lead we ask him/her to fill out our potential new client questionnaire and send us their last two years of accounts. We score their answers. If they score high enough we book in a short 15-minute conversation via the phone to check that we would be a good fit for them. Only after this conversation will I then go and meet them to bring them on board as a client.

As a result of this qualification process we probably qualify out half of our leads every month. It may sound quite high, but we find that the nearer the lead is to our client personas, the better a client they become for us.

—

When you are qualifying a client, and before you spend large amounts of time writing a proposal, you want to be finding out about the following four things, or DUFF:

- Decision maker

- Urgency

- Fit

- Funds

DECISION MAKER

Very often the person who enquires about using your firm's advisory services is not the ultimate decision maker. Whilst they may seem to have the right title to make the decision, it may not always be the case. For example, owner-managed businesses often need the approval of a husband or wife before they can commit to a large or unforeseen spend. As much as possible, your firm needs to be talking to the individuals who are the budget holder, and have the authority to allocate funds.

URGENCY

When someone buys a service from an accountant this normally represents a considered purchase. There is a high level of risk (be it money or reputation) as a result of using your firm's services. Therefore, before your firm allocates a large proportion of time to developing a piece of business, you need to make sure that the client intends to make a purchase and has a specific timeframe for doing so.

FIT

Not every Client and Accountant pairing will be a match made in heaven. And clients who have only taken compliance services from you before may become the client from hell, if they take advisory services from you.

When your firm first speaks to them, these needs may not be easily visible. In fact, the initial presenting problem is often not what, after some investigation, your firm ends up solving. You have to determine whether your client is truly interested to learn what is possible as a result of using your firm's advisory services, and is motivated to achieve this.

FUNDS

As early in the sales pipeline as possible you want to ascertain that the person has the financial capacity or access to the funds to buy advisory services from your firm. If they state that they don't have a budget for your firm's advisory services, this may not be a Game Over moment, but it does indicate that you will need to decide whether you want to educate them as to the value of your firm's advisory services. In an early conversation with a client it often helps to let them know what your firm's advisory services are likely to cost. In this early conversation, try not to be too prescriptive with your firm's fees, but do let your client know the likely range of fees that they may need to fork out for advisory services. For example:

Clients with problems similar to yourself typically find that it will cost them between £5k and £10k a year.

Once you have decided that your client is a good candidate for taking advisory services from your firm, you will then need to run a sales meeting. The next part of the chapter looks at how to structure and run a sales meeting with your client.

HOW TO STRUCTURE AND RUN A SALES MEETING

To help you and your firm get the best possible result from a sales meeting, follow this structure:

Before you meet:

- Agree time, date, duration and venue.

- [*For new clients to the firm*] Have a quick 10–15 minute phone call to qualify them

- Establish a loose agenda for the meeting.

- Ideally, send them a couple of pieces of valuable content which demonstrate your firm's expertise and authority.

- [For new clients to the firm] If you can, start a dialogue with them on social media.

A week before you meet:

- Check the meeting is still going ahead, and re-confirm time, date and venue.

- Check the agenda is still the same. Is there anything new that you or they have thought of that you need to include?

- Ask them whether there is anything that you need to prepare to help them get value from the meeting.

- Send them another piece of short valuable content, relevant to your meeting.

When you meet:

- [For new clients to the firm] Introduce yourself very briefly, i.e. in under a minute.

- Things may have changed since you last checked, so clarify how much time they have for the meeting, that the agenda is still appropriate, and what they want to achieve by the end of the meeting.

- Explain that you are keen to understand more about them, and the organisational reasons behind this meeting taking place, particularly *what has motivated them to talk to you today?*

- Allocate **at least 50%** of the meeting time to listen and explore their problems.

- Summarise to check understanding of what you are hearing.

- Identify the risks for the client of doing nothing, plus the value your firm can bring to the client by working with them.

- [*If a new client to the firm*] Find out the criteria that they will use to select a new accountant.

- Uncover their timings and anything that will affect their ability to proceed quickly.

- Suggest some potential solutions, and cost these solutions if requested.

- Find out any resistance or objections they may have to working with you.

- Agree any next steps and ask when they would like you to follow up with them if you have not heard anything.

After you meet:
- Thank them for their time.

- Send a note summarising your understanding of what was discussed.

- Do your next steps from the meeting.

- Diarise when you should contact them next.

How to increase your client's motivation to buy, particularly advisory services

As mentioned earlier in the chapter, unlike compliance services, your client does not *need* to buy advisory services. It is an optional spend. Consequently, in the sales meeting you need to increase your client's motivation to buy. Your client will only buy if they are experiencing a **pain point**. Fortunately (or unfortunately) most businesses are! This pain point can be strategic, financial, or personal pain, or a mixture of all three.

Examples of strategic pain:
- Growing pains

- Lack of decent leads

- A local competitor is undercutting them and taking away chunks of their business

Examples of financial pain:

- Poor profitability

- Cashflow problems

- Want to sell the business but the capital value on exit is not high enough to make it worth their while

Examples of personal pain:

- Working long hours

- High stress levels

- Not getting enough income out of the business to fund their current or future lifestyle

- Bored of running their business

Here is how you uncover their pain points in a sales meeting.

Your client is currently in the "as-is" state. The first thing your questioning needs to do is establish the "to-be" state. What are their goals and aspirations? What is really important for them to achieve and why? If they had a magic wand that they could wave to change something specific about their business, what would it be? Don't dismiss this line of questioning – it's very relevant, and may be the most important part of your meeting.

Once you have helped them identify their to-be state, the next part of the process is to accurately measure the distance between their as-is and the to-be state. The client will often have an inaccurate idea of how difficult it will be to achieve their desired state, and it'll be necessary for you to bring them down to earth and "increase the distance" between their as-is and to-be. After all, if it was easy to get to the to-be state, they wouldn't need your firm's advisory services.

Good questions to use to find out about the to-be state are:

- What motivated you to set up your business? How does your current reality match with this?

- What is your business trying to achieve? How will that benefit you personally?

- If you could sort out [problem/challenge] what would that mean for you personally and your business?

- What will become easier or better when you have achieved your business's goals?

- How will your life be better or easier when your business gets there?

- If your business achieves its goal, how will that impact your partner and family?

- What will doubling the capital value of your business on exit mean for your pension pot and future retirement?

- What's the motivation behind trying to achieve ...?

If you don't increase this distance in the sales meeting you will typically hear your client say things like:

- It's not a priority for us right now.

- We don't have the budget or cash flow for this.

- We think we can probably do this in-house.

Once you've increased the distance between a client's as-is and to-be it's then important for you to ground your client in reality. *Perhaps you could tell me a little about your situation*. Going back to their as-is brings your client back down to Earth with a big bump. This is your moment to really dig into their current as-is. For example:

- Tell me about your profits and losses

- Is this how you envisioned life would be as your own boss?

- How much longer do you think you can carry on with the way things are at the moment? What would be the implications if you didn't change anything?

- Are you spending enough quality time with your wife/husband/family?

- Do you really have enough profit to take the income you want out of the business?

- What have you tried and failed with?

- What are the weak links in your current organisation?

- What will happen if you can't overcome ...?

- What is the impact if you do nothing or delay with ...?

The idea of this is **not** to frighten or manipulate your client. *It is to give them an accurate picture of their business reality.* When you are digging into the as-is with your client, it is important for them to be challenged in order to not be in denial about what is really going on for them right now. If you do this stage right you will be able to pinpoint the pain they are feeling right now.

By increasing the distance between their as-is and to-be, and revealing the reality of the pain they are experiencing right now, you stand the best chance of your client naturally agreeing that your firm's advisory services being the solution they need to their problems.

—

GUY ROBINSON'S GROWTH STORY

My firm was one of the very early adopters of the cloud. It's helping us get to the point where we, as a firm, can truly deliver a real-time accounting service to our clients. This is often the reason clients opt to work with us. We received an enquiry from a supplier of one of our clients who was impressed with how they did all their finances in the cloud. Naturally, we had set up our client to work this way.

When I received the enquiry I thought, from my initial conversation to qualify the enquiry, there was the likelihood of a £10,000 annual recurring fee as they wanted Bookkeeping, Year End Accounts, Tax Returns and Management Accounts. In the business development meeting with the potential client it became apparent that their current accountant had got their business up onto the cloud but had made a huge mess of it. As a result, they were stuck. Their records were incorrect and they couldn't move forward with growing their business because they didn't have decent management information. Their pain point was huge and was really hurting them. They also didn't trust their current accountants to sort out the mess without another big bill.

As a result of investigating their pain points and the aspirations for their business, the client ended up agreeing a £21,000 annual recurring fee and a one-off fee of £2,000 for me to go up to their offices to sort out their systems. If I hadn't have spent so much time digging into their as-is and to-be I doubt I would have come away with such a big fee from the client.

When it comes to proposing a solution to your client, you want to make sure that you **turn the features of your advisory service into benefits for the client**. A feature is a fact about you or your firm's service – you can't deny it exists – whereas a benefit is something that your firm can do for the client, that the client wants. **Clients are typically buying into the benefits of your firm's service, rather than its features,** and it's important that they see the benefits of your firm as something that helps them solve their pain points.

When you understand the benefits that they really want and need, then you can tailor the features to help move your client to commit to buying advisory services from your firm. You can also propose solutions to help your client achieve their desired results. However, many accountants often struggle with features and benefits. Table 11.0 turns often used features into benefits.

Feature	Restated as a Benefit	Pain point solved
We are a local firm of accountants.	We are a local firm of accountants, which means that we are close enough to make it easy to have a face-to-face meeting when this is needed.	I'll be looked after, and they're close by if I need them
We are the only specialists for retail businesses in the area.	We are the only specialists for retail businesses in the area, which means that we are working with similar clients to you every day. We know the strategies which will help you grow your retail business, which KPIs to monitor like a hawk and which apps you can use in your business to take the headache out of your accounts and books.	As a retail business, I understand that my accountants are used to working with and solving the problems I deal with in my day-to-day
We are a small firm.	We are a small firm, which means that you will be a very important and major client to us, and receive a high level of personalised client service.	I'll be valued and won't be ignored

Table: Turning a feature into a benefit

The best way of finding out what is really important to your client, in order to turn a feature into a benefit, is to **ask them**. For example:

- If we work with you on this [problem], what is the main result you want to achieve?

- What is motivating you to solve this [problem]? What will solving it enable you to do?

WHAT TO DO IF YOU ARE FACED WITH DIFFICULT QUESTIONS FROM YOUR CLIENT?

Unfortunately, good results with your clients are never guaranteed. You know that, and any potential or current client knows that. Consequently, whenever a client decides to buy advisory services from your firm they will be risking their money, reputation and potential livelihood. As a consequence, they are always going to want to check out exactly what is involved in buying advisory services from your firm, and whether they believe that you can deliver what they want. When you are meeting your clients, you need to surface these concerns and ask potentially difficult questions.

Luckily, there are only three main reasons why a client will decide not to buy advisory services from your firm:

- They don't believe your firm is capable of doing the advisory work.

- They don't believe that they are getting good enough value if they buy advisory services from your firm

- There is not a good relationship fit.

When you realise this, it becomes a little easier to anticipate client concerns, and how these will be articulated. For example, if you were asked *What sort of results you have achieved with previous clients?*, this is the client testing your capability to be able to help them. Answer the difficult questions by using an example of how you have helped a similar type of client.

Whilst these difficult questions may not feel like it at the time, these are not because your client is being awkward, but normally they either want to be reassured about something or to find out the answer to something. Changing your mindset, to view difficult questions as just a request for more information, helps you be more relaxed in a sales meeting. It also helps you see that things like *Your fees are quite pricey* as a signal that they are thinking that the price is higher than your competition.

A good technique to use to help identify what are your client's objections to buying advisory services from your firm, is to proactively tell them some of the objections that other clients had before they were signed up. For example:

Although our costs are higher, all of our clients have remarked after implementation that they now realise that our solutions are robust, and therefore there is no tidy-up or refinement necessary afterwards.

When faced with one of these difficult questions, you want to let them know that not only do you understand why they feel that way, but that they are right, and others have in the past felt that way. In other words you are not being defensive, but reinforcing the fact that they are right. (Remember the client is the one who controls the buying process, and whether you disagree with what they are saying, they are the ones who will ultimately decide to hire you.) However, you also need to show them that clients who had been in exactly their situation, had managed to gain a positive outcome by working with you. This is called the **Feel, Felt, Found technique**.

Feel: I understand how you feel about paying to create a business plan with us.

Felt: Many of my other clients when they were in the same situation as you, felt the same way, and were wondering whether they pay to do a business plan with us, or just get on with themselves. They were really concerned about whether we would be able to add anything to the process.

Found: However, when we have worked with clients in exactly the same place as you now, they have commented about how much richer the business planning process was with us. They found our external, objective perspective, and the business planning process we used, enabled them to build a more complete, energising and realistic business plan than one they could do themselves. They were thrilled that they got more buy-in to the business plan by bringing their whole leadership team to the business planning workshop we ran for them.

Identifying the real barriers to using your firm's advisory services

Within the sales meeting, your aim is to find a mutually agreeable solution to your client's requirements. Whilst they may raise many objections to using your firm's advisory services, some of these may not hinder them signing on the dotted line. Your aim is to investigate which objections are 'real' and how to find a solution that works for both parties.

A great technique for doing this is the *If ... then ...*technique. Essentially, what you are saying with this technique is, 'That's an important issue, so **if** we can resolve it to your satisfaction, **then** we can proceed?' For example:

If we can find a way of reducing our coaching fees by 25 percent, will you then be happy to sign up for business coaching with the firm?

What happens if a client wants you to reduce your fees?

Even if you have qualified your client correctly, there are still times when they will ask for a reduction in your fees. Unless you are in a competitive bidding situation, this isn't a showstopper. Often, it's a very good indication that you are about to sign them up.

Your aim at this stage of the process is not to arbitrarily reduce your fees, as this is signalling to your client that every time they want a fee reduction, they just need to ask and your firm will do it. Instead, you need to establish *exactly* the value you are delivering to them; i.e. what it is that they really want, and what is non-essential. If you can cut the non-essentials from your packaged offering, then you can offer your client a more bespoke package at a reduced fee. Your client is happy, and you are happy because you have signed up a client and not reduced your firm's profit margin or devalued what your firm does for clients.

If you don't have the option to trim away parts of what your firm will do for the client, you may find that one of these approaches may help eliminate the deadlock:

- **Explain that the fee is what it is**, and if they don't want to pay this fee you will happily walk away, no hard feelings. Sometimes this works, and they still sign up.

- **Restate the benefits of using your firm's advisory services** and how this will help them achieve their organisational goals.

- **Demonstrate to them why it costs so much** and why you don't have the room to reduce your fees.

- **See whether they would accept a more junior member of staff working on their account**, in order to reduce the fee level.

- **Use a client story** to illustrate how other clients have also had doubts about your fees, but achieved great results, which justified your firm's fee.

TIPS FOR WRITING A PROPOSAL

It is unusual for a client to take advisory services without asking for a proposal. The invitation to write a proposal often brings you one step closer to a new client. A proposal, in its simplest form, is where you state what services your firm will provide, your firm's fees for doing so, and the objectives for working together. The form that your proposal takes could range from a simple email outlining what you and the client have agreed to do, to a full War and Peace-sized document for a formal tender process. Here are some tips for making sure your proposals get accepted:

Send your proposal to your client within 24 hours of the business development meeting

The sooner your client can receive your firm's proposal, the quicker they can sign it off. Often, new clients to the firm are really impressed if their potential new accountant can get them a proposal within 24 hours, as this is far from the norm. Software such as Practice Ignition or GoProposal will help your firm automate the proposal process. Clients are more likely to accept a proposal if it mirrors what you were talking about in the meeting. There should be no surprises. If you can use your firm's pricing tool with the clients in the meeting, this will help reduce any friction in accepting your firm's proposal.

Quantify the results the client can expect from engaging your firm

Your client is buying results. Therefore, quantify as much as possible the likely results you expect they will get if they work with your firm. Ensure that these results are linked to the client's goals and aspirations.

Use a proposal document template

Having standard templates within your firm can help you and your team quickly produce a proposal for a client. Wherever possible, use the firm's proposal document template to help you structure your proposal and cut down the time to write. However, do make sure that you tailor any standard pieces of text in the template to fit the piece of work your firm is bidding to win.

Keep the options to a minimum

It can be very tempting to present your client with a myriad of options and solutions in your proposal. This can have a similar effect to going into a shop, and being so overwhelmed by choice, that you get stuck in the decision making, consequently walking out of the shop having not bought what you originally intended to buy. Do not be tempted to give your client multiple options for advisory services in a proposal. Your proposed solution for advisory services needs to have been agreed upfront in the sales meeting. If your client hasn't agreed to buy advisory services from your firm in the sales meeting, they are not going to buy them just because you include them in the proposal!

Make sure that the proposal is readable

The proposal that you write should be simple and easy to read. Remember that your client may not be an expert in what your firm does, so eliminate jargon from the document. As you write the document, imagine you are sitting opposite the person and having a conversation. Aim to keep the tone of the document conversational, rather than dry, stilted and stuffed with corporatese.

Features and benefits

Wherever possible, go through your proposal document and turn any feature into a benefit for the client. The three main benefits that your client will be interested in are:

• Saving them time

• Saving them money

• Reducing their risk in hiring you.

For example, instead of stating, *We are the local expert* for ...,turn this into, *You know you will be in safe hands with us as we are the local expert* for ...

Differentiate your firm

If you know that your client is considering working with other accountants or professionals, then you need to make sure your proposal articulates why the client should choose your firm, rather than your competitors. However, you need to do this in way that doesn't rubbish your competitors. When you are speaking with your client, find out their top buying criteria for selecting who they work with. Then show in your proposal how your firm meets or exceeds these buying criteria.

Summary

A client will not buy advisory services from your firm until:

• There is enough internal urgency to want to spend money to solve their problems

• They have the budget to work with your firm

Your role in the sales meeting is to get a detailed understanding of your client's problems and propose a solution that your client is motivated to buy. To do this you will need to find their pain points. The best way to find their pain points is to accurately increase the distance between their as-is and to-be states, whilst pinpointing the pain they feel right now. When you propose a solution to your client make sure that you turn any features of your firm's services into benefits for your client.

17

WORKING TOGETHER: VIRTUAL CFO + CLIENT

WOOP are one of the fastest growing startups in the meal-kit delivery space in New Zealand. Since opening their doors three years ago, they've been working with Oxygen Advisors, an Auckland practice that specialises in advisory and virtual CFO (vCFO) services, supporting startup and high-growth companies.

Thomas Dietz, CEO of WOOP, and Matt Dold, Director of Oxygen Advisors, talk about how the advisor-client relationship has helped WOOP achieve pin-point control of cash flow, and how it supports their stratospheric growth. It's a great example of advisory services in action.

THE ROLE OF THE VIRTUAL CFO

Virtual CFO is a new and occasionally contentious term. Some in the industry suggest that the idea of an absent CFO doesn't exactly fill them with confidence, as a good CFO needs to know the businesses they support particularly well. But to Matt, the proof is in the success Oxygen has been able to help create for the businesses they support.

"Our clients raised almost 25% of the early stage seed capital invested in the New Zealand tech sector in 2017. Part of their ability to raise this capital is through having access to high quality, meaningful financials," Matt says.

Oxygen have grown to a team of six staff, working with over 30 high-growth companies – a ratio of one senior staff member to every 10 clients. Compared to a traditional CA firm, where each partner might be responsible for anywhere from 500 to 1000 clients (or more), Oxygen's emphasis is on providing personal, bespoke advice to the dynamic companies they support. The Oxygen team typically work onsite with each client for a day or two a month, although some clients require less time and some much more.

"Tools like Xero have opened a special opportunity for more advisory-focused CAs to really do a better job of advisory services," Matt says.

"It allows us to focus on strategy and delivering the best financial advice – whether that is related to monthly reporting, or to bigger projects such as raising capital."

THE OXYGEN-WOOP RELATIONSHIP

WOOP have an internal bookkeeper who comes in once a week to do reconciliations. Oxygen then carry out a sense check, making sure that the numbers are reliable and clean, and that the foundations are all correct in Xero. From there Matt will work with WOOP's different team members, talking over every aspect of the business's financials, and then use this foundation to project forward.

"We'll run through the results, look at the margins, check for any exceptions, understand where things have gone well – or not – of where we spent more than we thought we should, or whatever the case is," Matt says. "But the most important part is then looking forward and saying, 'Okay, what does this mean for the future?'"

THE BENEFITS OF A VIRTUAL CFO

"The main advantage of a vCFO is that it allows a young company to have access to the strategic thinking a CFO provides, without having to support the costs," says Thomas. "Alongside that, Xero allows us to spend much less time on basic accounting functions. It makes bookkeeping easy and painless, and allows us to focus our resources on strategy, looking forward rather than in the rear mirror."

Matt Dold cites a recent example where WOOP and Oxygen worked together to plan for an impending premise upgrade. The Oxygen team helped understand when WOOP would reach capacity in their current premises, then built detailed budgets and plans that covered operational and capital expenditure, and helped make sure that there was enough working capital and cash flow to support the move. The move was a significant milestone for WOOP, and having the support of a finance professional who intimately knew and understood the business model helped make this project achievable.

"We're helping make those business decisions using sound accounting information rather than just gut feeling," Matt says. "Often entrepreneurs like to make gut feel decisions, which sometimes work out – but often don't."

"In the past, young companies would have started with a bookkeeper, later adding a financial controller, before being able to hire a CFO, sometimes years down the track," adds Thomas. "The virtual CFO approach allows young companies to gain access to CFO-level advice at a much earlier stage than they have been able to in the past."

—

WHAT SERVICES MAKE UP A VIRTUAL CFO OFFERING?

An advisor offering virtual CFO services can assist a startup business in a number of vital ways. Thomas Dietz lists the key areas in which Oxygen has positively impacted WOOP on their journey so far:

1. **Assisting in defining a clear capital-raising strategy**. This has allowed WOOP to maximise their business growth and shareholders' return, while understanding the challenges and constraints that capital raising can bring.

2. **Setting up the right dashboards to manage cashflow**. Running out of cash is one of the higher risks startups face when they grow *really* fast. From day one, Oxygen has made sure that cashflow management has been an essential element of WOOP's operating processes. This has included weekly and monthly cash flow forecasting, as well as longer-term planning.

3. **Setting leading KPIs aligned directly with the business financial performance**. Financial and non-financial KPIs are constantly being reviewed and refined to ensure optimum business performance.

4. **Ongoing financial forecasting and capex planning**. This provides an insight into how and where future funds should be spent to ensure there are no nasty surprises down the line. Thomas and Matt work together every month to update the forecasts, reassess the plans, and make sure that all decisions are being made based on accurate and up-to-date information.

5. **Ongoing financial risk management**. Setting controls in place to manage the financial risks of the company, which otherwise might be overlooked.

6. **Monthly management reports/meetings**. Providing regular reports which look at both historical and future information. WOOP also gets the support of having a vCFO present at board meetings and strategy sessions, providing feedback across the business.

7. **Strategic thinking**. A vCFO is not just an accountant – but a real strategic partner, constantly supporting the CEO in their relatively lonely role by asking the right questions and helping them refine their thinking.

A SNAPSHOT OF ACCOUNTING'S FUTURE

"You hear every day that accountants are becoming more advisory, rather than compliance driven," Matt says. "I think accountants will still need to do compliance for a while – but maybe it's different for us, in that we do very little compliance."

Matt says tools like Xero, and other cloud accounting systems apps, have allowed him to really understand his clients' businesses, and operate as if they are a part of the management team.

"That's a massive change from years gone by," Matt states. "Through having access to information on a regular and up-to-date basis, I know exactly how WOOP is doing. I can really understand their business, and give meaningful advice that is actually useful for their business."

Thomas says that having a virtual CFO has been instrumental to WOOP's success to date, and that it wouldn't be possible without the quality and frequency of accounting advice they get from Oxygen.

"I'm happy to say we quadrupled the size of the business last year," he says. "We like having a virtual CFO. He's not too virtual, in that he assists us in real life. It's a really good relationship, and it's of great value to us."

Thomas adds that it's important to pick someone who really understands your business, is passionate about it, and wants to provide value.

"If they don't understand your area of business, then they're not the right person for you. It's such an intimate relationship that they really need to know the industry quite well."

Matt agrees, adding that advisors should place a premium on having the right data to make the right decisions – and familiarity with the industry or niche means decisions can be better informed.

"Like Thomas says, use advisors that are passionate about your business, that really want to help, and that really understand your industry, to help provide the information so you can make informed decisions."

ABOUT WOOP

WOOP is on a mission to empower its customers to live their best life, every night.

On Sundays, WOOP delivers everything its customers need to cook three or four dinners for the week. What makes WOOP different from any other food kit on the market? They do all the preparation in advance: veggies are diced, sauces and dressings are handmade in advance and meats are marinated. This ensures customers can cook dinners very easily, in half the time it would normally take.

"Our customers love being able to create homemade meals for their family, and only spend half the time in the kitchen - because with WOOP they've essentially got a sous-chef doing the prep," says Dietz.

The secret sauce is that unlike other meal-kit companies, WOOP caters for busy professionals who don't always have time to spend an hour in the kitchen, cooking a meal from scratch. It's the perfect option for those who like to live fast but eat slow.

ABOUT OXYGEN ADVISORS

Oxygen offers a wide spectrum of advisory services as part of their headline virtual CFO service, including monthly reporting and forecasting, capital raising, business plan development, market entry, mentoring and exit planning. With their clients having raised 25% of the early stage seed money raised in the New Zealand tech sector in 2017, Oxygen is well placed to provide experience, knowledge and networks to early-stage companies.

Having tripled in size in 2018, Oxygen's team works with most of New Zealand's most promising high-growth companies. A core part of their ethos is maintaining a high-touch approach to all their clients. Oxygen has a ratio of one vCFO to every 10 clients, with further support staff on top of that. Compared to a traditional CA firm, where each partner might be responsible for anywhere from 500 to 1000 clients, Oxygen's emphasis is on providing personal, bespoke advice to the dynamic companies they support. The Oxygen team typically work onsite with each client for a day or two each month, although some clients require less time and some much more.

"An average day might be spent counselling on anything from capital raising through to cash flow forecasting, but often extends out to blue sky conversations around changes in their industry, or new trends overseas," explains Matt.

Oxygen operates the way an in-house CFO would, outsourcing as much compliance as possible to a general CA firm, preferring to offer their services as advisors and in-house bookkeepers instead.

"We're more than happy for a company to continue their relationship with their existing CA," Matt says. "For a lot of our clients, it's quite good to have that 'Big Four' stamp on the front of the end-year accounts — especially if they're raising capital. We're happy for one of the Big Four to do that, while we'll focus on managing the internal side of things."

—

VIRTUAL CFO SERVICES HELP KEEP MARKETING SMART

WOOP's General Manager Operations, William Lockie says that having Oxygen on board helps them understand exactly how they're performing on a weekly, monthly, and yearly basis. This is especially helpful when it comes to something that's becoming ever more data driven: marketing.

"We can forecast our marketing spend, know where we can pull back, and where we can invest more. It provides the accountability needed to make sure that we are quite structured with how we choose to invest funds," Will says.

This year, WOOP have far outpaced their growth expectations. Having Oxygen provide structure and accountability means that they are able to re-forecast based on up-to-date numbers and, whenever warranted, reinvest their revenue into pursuing rapid growth.

"So, rather than say, 'No, we've set our marketing budget for the year,' we can quickly make the call to invest our additional revenue in further growth," Will says.

"It's allowed us to really drive our marketing, and ramp up the revenue growth. Having your fingers more on the pulse means that you can react far faster, and minimise mistakes while also maximising opportunities."

—

CONCLUSION

Right as we were finishing this book, a timely news story appeared. Chartered Accountants Australia and New Zealand (CAANZ) had just completed a survey that told a tale many accountants already know: that the top three skills for accountants over the coming years would be adaptability, emotional intelligence, and critical thinking. Also worth repeating is the fact that for the top 30 firms in Australia and New Zealand, advisory services topped the list of fastest-growing services. CAANZ chief executive Rick Ellis had a particularly noteworthy comment, worth reproducing in full:

As automation moves in, the communicators, the problem solvers and the adapters will take over. Human and technology skills will be even more in demand. Technology in particular is driving these changes, shifting the focus of work away from traditional skill sets of accountants, the numbers and the analytics. Instead, accountants are now using technology to free themselves up to add further value to businesses and take on a more strategic advisory role with clients. Our prediction is that in 2030 there will not be fewer accountants than there are now due to automation, but most will be doing very different work.

We couldn't think of a better way to sum up this book. As automation comes to industry after industry, and as the dust settles from disruption, it's often found that the work that's been automated hasn't actually gone away – but that it has vastly changed.

This too, will be the case for accounting's transition to advisory. The opportunity is huge for those that seize it, as more and more businesses start buying new services from accountants that move to embrace advisory. Practices that don't take the opportunity to become advisors now run the risk of finding themselves either bought out, left behind, or gone entirely.

In this book, we've heard from some of the top minds in accounting, and some of the best pacesetting practices. Their experience proves that there's no need for pessimism about the state of the industry; transformation is possible, even for the oldest and most traditional firms, and the rewards are more than worth it, both for practices and their clients. For those that don't need convincing, and are simply looking for the best way to structure their advisory services, we hope that the examples already in this book will provide you with insights and frameworks on how to do just that.

No matter where your firm is at in its advisory journey – whether you're just now looking to offer business advice or you've got a practice full of virtual CFOs – the important thing is that you're taking steps; that you're talking to clients, and helping them achieve their goals. The structures, tools and frameworks showcased in this book for doing this work are real and helpful, but if you keep "how can I best help my clients" at the centre of your practice, then you're an advisor.

One more thing

We hope this book has been valuable to you. What we want to know, just like all good advisors should, is how we can be more valuable to you – our partners. To that end, we genuinely want your feedback about this book: what you liked, what you didn't, your ideas, your nominations for other pacesetters, your winning strategies, your frameworks, tools, and stories. Especially your stories. The more we can share the successes of advisors, the more practices can benefit.

To let us know what you think, email the authors at **pacesetters@xero.com**. We will read everything you send us, and we can't wait to hear from you.

ABOUT XERO

"Xero is a New Zealand-based software company that develops cloud-based accounting software for small and medium-sized businesses."

That's what the Wikipedia description says about Xero, and it's about right – but wait, there's more.

Xero ushered in the cloud accounting revolution when it was founded by Rod Drury in 2006. The concept at the core of the software is that all financial data is stored in the cloud, on a single ledger, meaning all users see the same set of books no matter where they are in the world or what device they're using.

After refining its product in New Zealand, Xero software is now used in regions all over the world, in the UK, the US, Australia, Asia, South Africa, and Canada.

Our mission? Small business makes the world go round – it's the heart of the global economy. At Xero, we want millions of small businesses to thrive through beautiful software, great advice and connections. We know that small businesses do best when they're connected to an advisor.

This means an incredibly important part of Xero's mission is to help accounting and bookkeeping practices all over the world. We aim to make being a small business – or an accounting practice – more efficient and profitable, and more enjoyable too.

If you're new to Xero:
Four easy steps to get started

We'd love to have you on board. If you're not already a Xero partner, sign up to the Xero partner programme at **www.xero.com/partners** or get in touch with the team by emailing **partnerteam@xero.com**

Once you're on board, you'll be put in touch with your Xero account manager. From there, follow these four steps to get started with the cloud:

1. Free up time for talking with clients

Once you've decided that the cloud is the way forward for your practice, a Xero account manager is the perfect person to help you get underway. It's their job to help you with every aspect of the transition to the cloud and be there for you every step of the way.

2. Become the trusted advisor

Once you've become a Xero partner, getting you and your team certified is key to ensuring your practice understands Xero and how it can help your clients. The most successful partners are always the ones who have their team certified – so everyone is singing from the same sheet. Many practices adopt a "10 percent time" (or similar) model, where staff can use a percentage of their work hours entirely for getting certified on Xero. This quickly becomes productive, as certified staff are far more effective when helping clients or working on Xero-related tasks in the business.

3. Real-time equals real insights

We understand that making a significant change within your practice isn't an easy process, which is why we've launched migration certification. Migration certification is perfect for the person at your practice responsible for your migration project and is filled with guidance, resources and tools to support your practice's switch to the cloud.

4. Help clients free up their time

Of course, you need to keep your books current when you're changing software. You can easily move two years' worth of data from Sage and QuickBooks Desktop clients to Xero with Movemybooks, which is why it's used and recommended by many of our pacesetting practices.

ALL ABOUT THE XERO PARTNER PROGRAMME

The Xero partner programme is a way for you to be rewarded with a huge range of benefits you can tailor to your own practice goals. When you perform certain actions or hit particular milestones, you're rewarded with partner points. The more you earn, the higher your partner status level, and the more benefits you'll get. There are five levels of partnership:

1. Partner

2. Bronze partner

3. Silver partner

4. Gold partner

5. Platinum partner

You earn points for every client who either invites you into their Xero account, or for each client that you pay the Xero subscription for. You earn points for clients on Xero Business Edition, Xero Payroll, Xero Projects and Xero Expenses. Plus you get points for using some of our products for your own practice too.

You can also win Xero champion badges by checking off certain actions within your level of the Xero partner programme. For instance, to become a bronze champion, you need to have been a Xero partner for 12 months plus have achieved the bronze partner status level, earned 10 points or more in the past 12 months, and have at least two Xero certifications, with one being advisor certification.

Points and partner levels aren't just for show (although they're great for showing clients that you've got the expertise they need). There are a huge number of useful benefits that increasing your partner level can offer your practice – starting with discounts for Xero Business Edition that scale as you increase your level, and access to practice software like Xero Practice Manager, and Xero Workpapers. There are also great benefits like expert assistance with bulk client conversions, access to consulting and project support, and eligibility for marketing and event funding at higher levels.

Check out all the partner programme benefits and levels at **xero.com/uk/partners**

MEET YOUR XERO ACCOUNT MANAGER

Your Xero account manager is the personification of the relationship between Xero and accountants and bookkeepers. Think of them as your personal guide on the Xero journey – one with the tools to help you out every step of the way. There are plenty of places throughout this book where we advise getting in touch with your Xero account manager, and that's because they've already helped practices to solve problems or hurdle obstacles just like the ones you face.

Whether it's just getting started with Xero or building an advanced advisory practice, your Xero account manager is here to help. They can also introduce you to a wealth of resources, like educational content, certification, marketing funds, collateral and more, so you and your clients get the most out of Xero.

Co-authors

Josh Drummond

Josh has been a professional writer, journalist and marketer for over a decade, and works as a writer and content strategist for Xero. He currently talks to accountants for a living, which is much more interesting than it sounds. Josh is married and lives in Auckland, New Zealand. In his spare time, he has a variety of hobbies ranging from competitive punning to painting birds wearing hats.

Doug LaBahn, PhD.

Doug LaBahn leads Xero's global product and partner marketing. He has a PhD in marketing and is the author of Xero's partner benchmarking series and co-author of The Pacesetters. Doug has been leading innovation, research, marketing and partner programmes at global software, best practices and information services companies for over 20 years. He married his true love, Dana, right after he turned at 25. At age twenty-seven, Doug received his PhD and became university professor. He's been discovering and sharing the most effective ways to grow advisory firms serving small businesses ever since.

- doug.labahn@xero.com

- linkedin.com/in/doug-labahn

- Twitter: @douglabahn

Pacesetters

Shaye Thyer, BDO Australia

Shaye Thyer is the National Cloud and Advisory Specialist at BDO Australia. Recently named one of the top 50 most influential women in accounting, Shaye is spearheading BDO's move to cloud. She is a member of numerous accounting industry advisory bodies, including the Australian Xero Partner Advisory Council.

- linkedin.com/in/shayethyer/

Jason Ackerman, BNA CPA

Jason is a CPA that enjoys helping businesses become more profitable with the help of the right technology, accounting, and tax solutions. He loves thinking about how the world is changing and how he can keep my firm and my clients ahead of the curve.

When he's not accounting Jason enjoys playing piano in his band, watching and playing sports, and researching for a food blog maintained by him and his wife.

Chad Davis and Josh Zweig, LiveCA

Chad Davis helps run LiveCA from an office in the back of a luxury RV he shares with his wife and children. Co-founder Josh Zweig travels the world as he works, talking to clients from South America and taking time out at Burning Man. Live CA is a fully-remote firm offering cutting-edge advisory services, and Chad serves on a number of Canadian accounting industry boards and bodies.

Olly Evans, Evans & Partners

Olly is a partner at Evans and Partners, an award winning firm of chartered accountants in Bristol that has made a change from operating as a "compliance factory" to offering substantial advisory services. Evans & Partners were the first Xero Platinum Partner in the south west of the UK, and they are proud to have 97 percent of their clients recommend them, scoring their services 9.7 out of 10.

Neil Sinclair and Hamish Morrow, WK Advisors & Accountants

Neil joined WK in 2004 after over 10 years at a big four and he's been working in public practice for 25 years. Neil led WK's move to cloud accounting and advisory services and was recognised as Xero MVP in 2014 and the Mindshop Rising Star Award in 2017.

Outside work Neil loves to spend family time with his wife Mil, and girls Maddy and Jes. They enjoy going fishing in the Sounds and mountain biking.

Providing businesses with the tools they need to be successful is a passion for Hamish Morrow. Specialising in management accounting and information systems, he strives to help clients improve their management information by keeping up to date with all the latest in business technology and software.

He also plays golf and loves spending time with his wife Emma and their two sons.

CONTRIBUTORS

Will Farnell

Will is the founder of FarnellClarke, an innovative and pioneering accounting firm based in Norwich and London, UK. He set up Farnell Clarke in 2007 having previously worked within a Big Four firm advising predominantly public sector bodies on efficiency and process improvement. From day one he had a desire for Farnell Clarke to be a different kind of accounting firm.

Under Will's leadership the firm's seen consistent growth averaging 36% year on year for the last 10 years. The firm has twice been named Best Independent Firm (East of England) at the British Accountancy Awards, and in 2016 was named Most Innovative Firm in the independent and overall categories.

Will now uses the experiences acquired over the last 10 years as a tech-driven firm to support other firms in moving to a digital-based strategy.

- willfarnell.com
- linkedin.com/willfarnell
- Twitter: @willfarnell

Richard Clark

Richard is founder and CEO of Spotlight Reporting, Xero's number 1 reporting and forecasting app partner globally, and App Partner of the Year in 2015 and 2016. Spotlight Reporting now has 50 staff in Australia, the UK, the US and New Zealand.

Richard was previously the General Manager of Xero Workpapers (2012-14), a software business acquired by Xero. Richard has been an active Board Member of other companies, an investor and is the author of the Transform! Advisory Playbook.

Richard was in active public practice as a Chartered Accountant and Advisor until 2010, focusing on Virtual CFO and strategic services with a penchant for technology clients.

- spotlightreporting.com
- linkedin.com/in/richardfranciswgtnnz/
- Twitter: @RFrancisWellyNZ

James Mason

James Mason has over 20 years' experience supporting leading professional service firms and consultants around the world grow successful advisory businesses.

As Managing Director of the global learning and development network Mindshop, he oversees the training, coaching, resource development, emerging advisory technology, and growth needs of over 1000 advisors and business leaders who are part of the Mindshop community.

His experience provides him with unique insight into what works and what doesn't in the successful delivery of business advisory services to any sized business, anywhere in the world.

- mindshop.com
- linkedin.com/in/jamesmason8888/
- Twitter: @MindshopOnline

James Solomons

James Solomons' area of expertise focuses on the technological revolution taking place and its impact on SMEs & the role of accountants in the new digital landscape. He is CEO of Xref and is the former Xero Australia Head of Accounting.

James has over 17 years experience in public practice and after joining Xero in late 2014, made the decision to start a new 100 percent cloud based firm from scratch & co-founded Aptus Accounting & Advisory in January 2015 which has doubled in growth every year since its beginning. It was recognised as one of the Top 50 Cloud Accounting Firms in Australia by HubDoc in 2018 and in June 2018 won the Most Innovative Accounting Firm in Australia award at the Australian Accounting Awards.

He is a Fellow of Chartered Accountants Australia New Zealand (FCA), a graduate member of the Australian Institute of Company Directors (GAICD) a mentor, lecturer and industry partner at Macquarie University and has been actively involved in the community for much of his professional career.

- Aptusadvisory.com.au

- linkedin.com/in/jamessolomonsca/

- Twitter: @JamesSolomonsCA

Jason Andrew

Jason is a chartered accountant and has over a decade of experience as a business and corporate advisor, working with Government, mid cap and small businesses. He advises on a range of areas including mergers and acquisitions and transaction services, valuations, strategy and performance improvement. He also knows just enough about tax to be dangerous...

Jason is co-founder of SmartBooks Online, a bookkeeping and operational finance business servicing clients across Australia and the USA. By ensuring timely, accurate and robust accounting, SmartBooks Online handles the data entry process, providing a completely digitised and outsourced bookkeeping solution to SMBs.

Jason is passionate about helping business owners extract value from their numbers and data. His personal mission is to improve the financial literacy of entrepreneurs and change the current worldview of the accounting profession.

- smartbooksonline.com.au

- linkedin.com/in/jason-andrew/

- Twitter: @SmartBooks_Aus

Liz Farr

Liz Farr spent 15 years in tax and accounting at small firms in New Mexico, and has been a CPA since 2005. Besides focusing on tax returns of all flavours, she worked on audits of governmental entities and not-for-profits, business valuations, and litigation support. Since 2015, Liz has worked as a freelance writer specializing in content marketing for accountants and bookkeepers around the world. When she's not writing about accounting, Liz is skiing or hiking in the mountains of New Mexico (yes, it does snow in the high mountains here!)

- www.farrcommunications.com

- linkedin.com/in/liz-farr-5165244a

- Twitter: @liz_farr

Heather Townsend

Heather Townsend is the author and founder of the Accountants Millionaires' Club, and the award-winning and best-selling author of 5 books. Despite her mother not being able to vote, she regularly makes the top ten lists of influencers to the accountancy profession.

- accountantsmillionaire.club

- linkedin.com/in/heathertownsend

- Twitter: @heathertowns